THE DATA RECORDER

THE DATA RECORDER

Frank J. Clark

*Associate Professor of
Data Processing
Genesee Community College
Batavia, New York*

RESTON PUBLISHING COMPANY, INC., Reston, Virginia 22090

A Prentice-Hall Company

Library of Congress Cataloging in Publication Data

Clark, Frank James, 1922-
     The data recorder.

     1. Electronic digital computers—Programming.
2. Computer input-output equipment. I. Title.
QA76.6.C53   001.6'42   73-8933
ISBN 0-87909-178-9

PREFACE

The main objective of this text is to prepare the student for all types of data entry and verification possible in the Data Recorder. Further, after completion of this text students should have an understanding of the principles of Data Recorder operations.

The text:
1/ Develops an understanding of the nature of data collection.
2/ Describes how data is translated from source documents to electronic data representation.
3/ Develops understanding of the skills needed for machine operation.
4/ Provides a variety of data entry applications including payroll, accounts receivable, sales, and orders.

Teaching and learning aids that develop machine skills are found in exercises and problems at the end of most chapters, and in the sections dealing with error analysis and correction. Supplementary materials include Appendices containing speed drills and applications.

Frank J. Clark

CONTENTS

Chapter 1

INTRODUCTION

A *data recorder* is a device used to enter data from source documents onto a magnetic tape.

The source document, for example, a purchase order (Figure 1-1), is placed on the reading table at the left of the keyboard shown in Figure 1-2. The operator keys in the data from the source document onto a reel of magnetic tape. The data is recorded on the tape in the form of small magnetic spots.

The data recorder is also used to verify data, transmit data to another data recorder or receive data from another data recorder.

REQUISITIONER'S COPY

GENESEE COMMUNITY COLLEGE

COLLEGE ROAD / P. O. BOX 718

BATAVIA, NEW YORK 14020

P.O. No. 10581

Delivery Date 3/30

TO

All-Steel Equipment
P.O. Box 235
Fayetteville, New York

SHIP TO: GENESEE COMMUNITY COLLEGE
COLLEGE ROAD
BATAVIA, NEW YORK 14020
ATTN: CENTRAL RECEIVING DEPT.
Requested By: Frank Clark
Division   Data Processing

THE ABOVE P.O. NUMBER MUST APPEAR ON ALL
INVOICES, VOUCHERS, CORRESPONDENCE, ETC.
BILL ONE CLAIM PER PURCHASE ORDER.

DATE: Feb. 22   TERMS: ACCT. CODE:

ITEM	QUANTITY	DESCRIPTION	UNIT PRICE	UNIT	AMOUNT
		New York State Contract: 32512			
	1	Desk, Model 6655, Mojave Tan Dark Brown Molding (Round) Walnut Top	140.39		140.39
		New York State Contract: P32357			
	3	Swivel Chairs, Model 846 Black Frame, Avocado Fabric/Dallis Olive Vinyl, Standard Treatment	50.55		151.65
				TOTAL	292.04

REMARKS:

3/30 DATE   Wm Ireland (RECEIVER'S SIGNATURE)

APPROVAL OF OFFICIAL ORIGINATING CLAIM: I HEREBY CERTIFY THAT
THIS BILL HAS BEEN RENDERED IN ACCORDANCE WITH THE CONTRACT,
AGREEMENT, OR ACCEPTED ESTIMATE, AND THAT THE WORK HAS BEEN
COMPLETED AND/OR THE MATERIALS DELIVERED SATISFACTORILY.

3/20 DATE   F. J. Clark (DEPARTMENT APPROVAL)

FIGURE 1-1

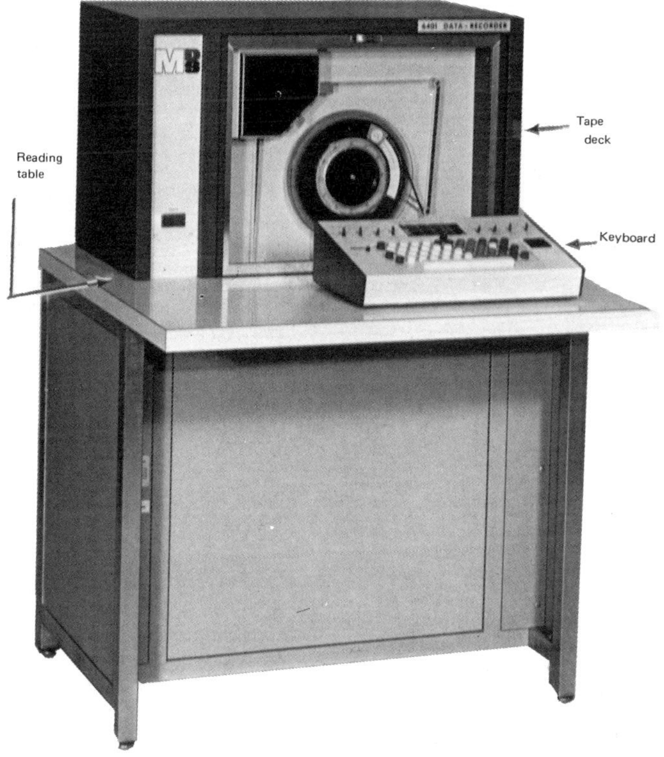

FIGURE 1-2   Courtesy of Mohawk Data Sciences Corp

Data on tape requires much less space than data keypunched into cards. A typical reel of tape can store an amount of data greater than the amount contained on 18,000 punched cards or 9 boxes of punched cards. Data transmission speeds are vastly increased using the data recorder. One of the fastest card readers transmits data to the computer at 2,000 cards per minute—based on the 80 column card, this is 160,000 characters per minute. A computer that uses tape input can read and store 1.3 million characters per minute.

In the text and exercises that follow reference is made to files, records, fields, data items, and characters of data. These are defined as follows:

A *file* is a collection of records which have common characteristics or functions. For example, a payroll file contains records of names, hours worked, and rates paid; an accounts receivable file contains records of customer names and purchases.

A *record* is a group of related items that is treated as a unit. For example, a bank deposit slip contains such items of data as the depositor's name and account number; the amount to be deposited, and the date.

A *data item* is a single piece of information which may be found in a record; for example, a name, number, amount, or date.

A *field* is one or more consecutive positions in the memory unit of the data recorder or on a reel of tape that is reserved for a data item (shown in Figure 1-3).

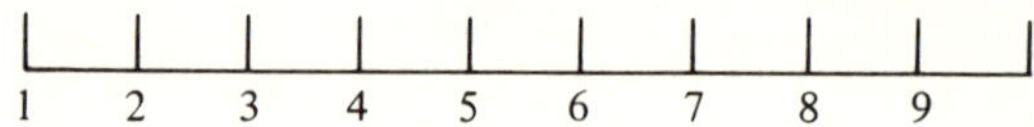

FIGURE 1-3

For example, Figure 1-3 shows a field of nine positions reserved for the data item called the social security number. Figure 1-4 shows the data item (social security number) entered into the nine-position field.

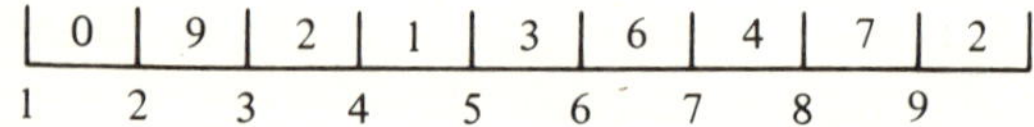

FIGURE 1-4

A *character* is a single symbol in a data item. This symbol may be any digit (0-9), any letter (A-Z), or a special symbol such as *, .$, etc. Digits are called numeric characters; letters are referred to as alphabetic characters and special symbols are referred to as special characters.

The data recorder is composed of three units, each of which must be understood by the operator. The units are the tape deck, the keyboard, and the magnetic core memory.

THE TAPE DECK

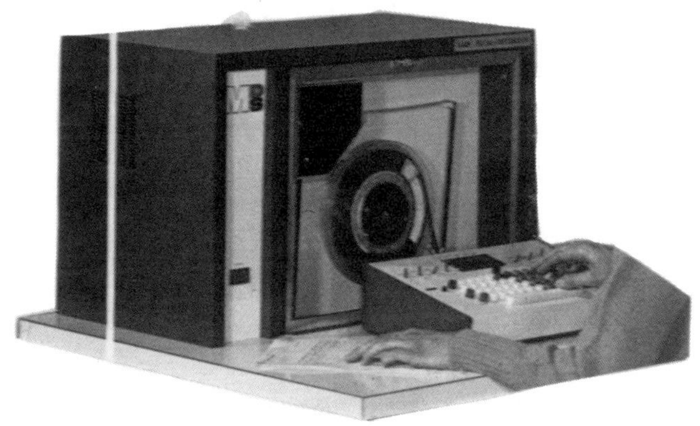

Courtesy of Mohawk Data Sciences Corp

FIGURE 1-5　The Tape Deck

The tape deck contains the magnetic tape reel, the master program tapes (pg. 101) and files, the read/write head, the erase head, and the tape feed mechanism.

The Tape Reels

The magnetic tape reel may be any IBM-compatible tape reel up to 10.5 inches diameter. Recording is done on a standard ½-inch wide magnetic tape with a character density of 800 characters per inch. This makes it possible to store the equivalent of ten punched cards, each containing 80 characters of information, in the space of one inch. A record on the data recorder may contain from 10 to 180 characters of information. There is no pick-up reel for the recorded tape. The recorded tape falls into an enclosed bin which is capable of holding approximately 1200 feet of tape. The operator (YOU) must always remember that care must be taken when handling magnetic tape to avoid scratching or stretching it.

MASTER PROGRAM TAPES

A program tape is a portion of magnetic tape approximately four feet in length that is used as a control over the keying of source data. Program tapes contain instructions to the data recorder to accept numeric or alphabetic characters for particular fields of data. Creation of program tapes is discussed in Chapter 8.

THE READ/WRITE AND THE ERASE HEAD

The functions of the read/write and the erase head are to verify data on the tape, write new data on the tape, and erase data on the tape. A read/write and an erase head are shown in Figure 1-6 as is a tape feed mechanism and mounting unit. The tape feed mechanism positions the tape for read and write operations and is discussed on page 44.

THE KEYBOARD

The keyboard is on the reading table in front of the tape deck. The keyboard may be moved around on the reading table by the operator to facilitate the keying operation. Source documents to be keyed onto tape are usually placed on the reading table to the left of the keyboard. The keyboard contains three units: data entry keys, function keys, control and display panel with control switches (see Figure 1-7).

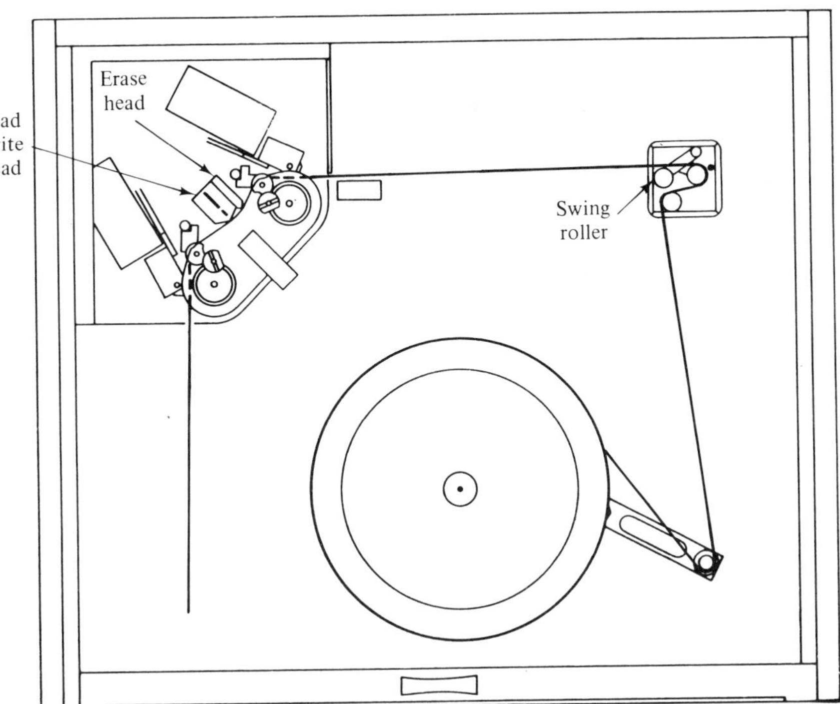

FIGURE 1-6

MAGNETIC CORE MEMORY

The magnetic core memory is the "brain" of the data recorder. It can be corrected or changed at the operator's command. It contains data being recorded or verified and the program instructions. There are two separate types of core memory: *data memory* and *program memory*. These are described as follows:

Data Memory

Each position in the data memory contains one character of information expressed in eight magnetic cores (or bits). Each core contains a bit of information expressed only as a 1 or 0. A core in the *ON* condition is considered to have a value of 1. A

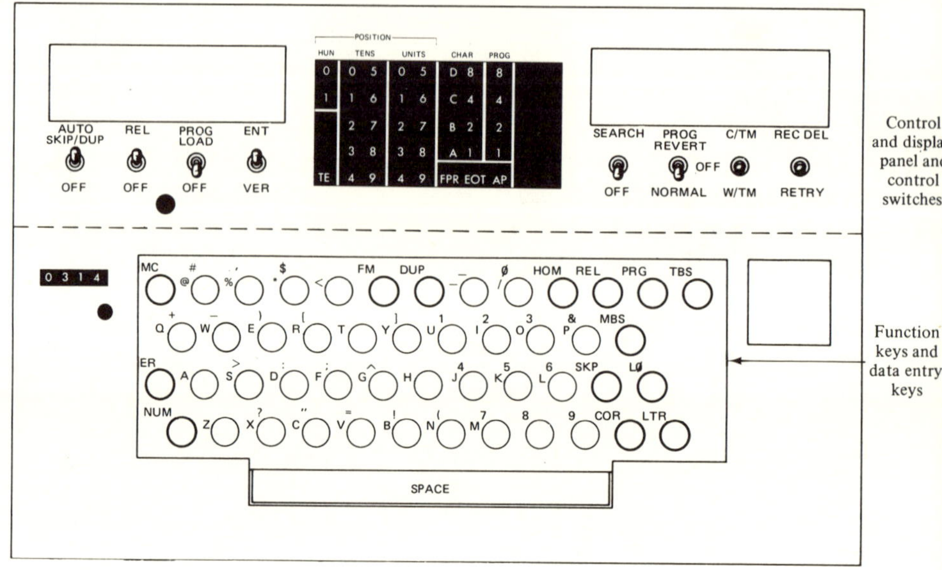

FIGURE 1-7

core in the *OFF* condition is considered to have a value of 0. An 8-bit position of memory is shown in the center column in Figure 1-8.

The dark cores are in the ON condition, the unshaded cores in the OFF condition. Each core has a name. These names are designated by the letters and digits DCBA8421.

When cores DCBA are in the ON condition and cores 8421 are in the OFF condition, the memory location (shown in Figure 1-8) represents the value of 0.

Other examples of particular cores in data memory are Z (Figure 1-9) and the special character * (asterisk) (Figure 1-10). A complete list of bit values is shown in Table 1-1. The values for each character is given in the right-hand columns of Table 1-1. These values, 1 and 0, represent numbers in the binary numeration system. It is not necessary to understand the binary numeration system to read characters found in data memory. It *is* important to know how to convert keyboard characters to the 8-bit EBCDIC code and back again using Table 1-1. Understanding this code enables recovery from errors keyed onto tape.

TABLE 1-1

6401 EBCDIC* Codes

Character	EBCDIC Code DCBA8421	Character	EBCDIC Code DCBA8421	Character	EBCDIC Code DCAB8421
A	11000001	V	11100101	!	01001111
B	11000010	W	11100110	&	01010000
C	11000011	X	11100111	[	01011010
D	11000100	Y	11101000	$	01011011
E	11000101	Z	11101001	*	01011100
F	11000110	0	11110000	)	01011101
G	11000111	1	11110001	;	01011110
H	11001000	2	11110010	∧	01011111
I	11001001	3	11110011	-	01100000
J	11010001	4	11110100	/	01100001
K	11010010	5	11110101	,	01101011
L	11010011	6	11110110	%	01101100
M	11010100	7	11110111	—	01101101
N	11010101	8	11111000	>	01101110
O	11010110	9	11111001	?	01101111
P	11010111	Space	01000000	:	01111010
Q	11011000	]	01001010	#	01111011
R	11011001	.	01001011	@	01111100
S	11100010	<	01001100	'	01111101
T	11100011	(	01001101	=	01111110
U	11100100	+	01001110	"	01111111
				MC	00000000

*Extended Binary Coded Decimal Interchange Code

Program Memory

The function of program memory is to give the operator control over the data recorder through the various program codes. The program codes are entered as numeric characters and are displayed as four binary digits.

The eight magnetic cores for program memory are shown in Fig. 1-11. Note that the *program memory* is divided into two

Core names	Cores	Value
D	●	1
C	●	1
B	●	1
A	●	1
8	0	0
4	0	0
2	0	0
1	0	0

FIGURE 1-8

Core names	Cores	Value
D	●	1
C	●	1
B	●	1
A	0	0
8	●	1
4	0	0
2	0	0
1	●	1

FIGURE 1-9

parts; one for *MAIN* program memory, the other for *ALTernate* program memory.

The four cores in each program memory position are specified as 8, 4, 2, and 1. Program codes are expressed in binary numbers using combinations of 1 and 0. The operator keys in a decimal number on the keyboard and the data recorder converts the decimal number into its *binary* equivalent. If the operator wishes to read a program code that is already in program memory and translate it into its decimal equivalent it is necessary to add up the decimal specifications for each core.

Core names	Cores	Value
D	0	0
C	●	1
B	0	0
A	●	1
8	●	1
4	●	1
2	0	0
1	0	0

FIGURE 1-10

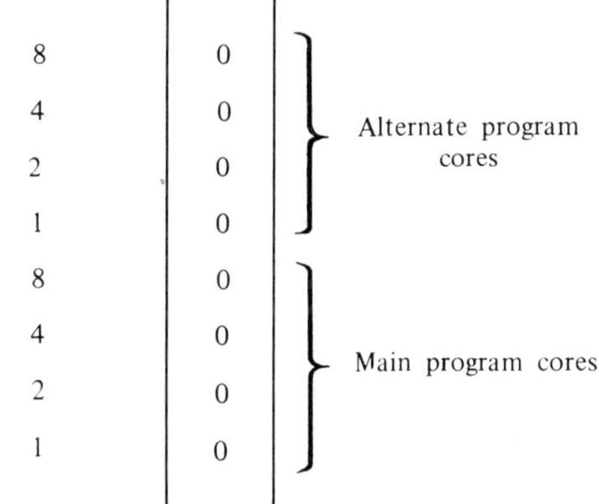

FIGURE 1-11

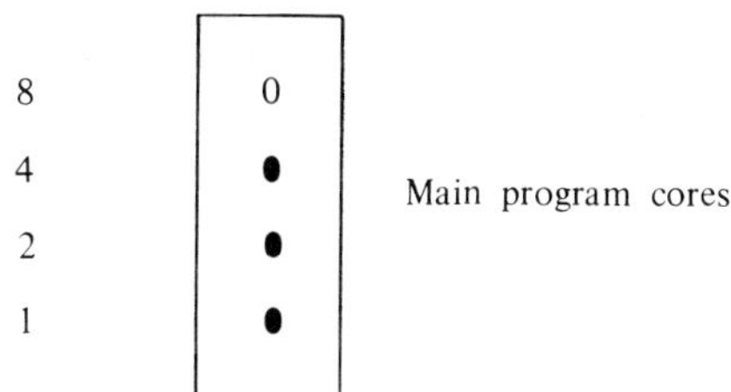

FIGURE 1-12

For example, the core shown in Figure 1-12 contains a seven since $4 + 2 + 1 = 7$.

The following table gives decimal numbers with their binary equivalents:

TABLE 1-2

Decimal	Binary Cores 8421
0	0000
1	0001
2	0010
3	0011
4	0100
5	0101
6	0110
7	0111
8	1000
9	1001
10	1010
11	1011
12	1100
13	1101
14	1110
15	1111

The program codes control data entry operations on the data recorder. The codes are entered into the data recorder through the keyboard or through a program tape.

These codes remain unchanged during an entry run and either *MAIN* or *ALTernate* memory may be selected by the operator. The first position of a field or *Most Significant Position* (MPS) may contain the program code that will stop any automatic machine action such as auto skip or auto dup. The code in the MPS will also put the machine in the appropriate shift mode for the data items that follow. Table 1-3 summarizes these codes and gives their binary equivalents.

TABLE 1-3

Program Codes

Program Code	Function	Binary Code
SP (space)	numeric shift	0000*
1	alpha shift	0001*
2	begin numeric	0010
3	begin alpha	0011
4	begin/end auto dup	0100
5	begin auto skip	0101
6	programmed left zero	0110
7	programmed left zero	0111

The two basic operations of the data recorder are:

1. Recording data on tape and

2. Verification of data on tape.

RECORDING DATA ON MAGNETIC TAPE

1. The operator keys a record from a source document into a *memory* unit. If the operator senses an error at this time it is corrected by backspacing and rekeying the corrected data.

2. When all data items pertaining to a record are entered, the operator sends the record from the memory unit to the magnetic tape.

3. The data-recorder then automatically backspaces the tape and then moves the tape forward and compares the data to the contents of the memory unit to insure that all characters were transmitted correctly.

*will not stop skip/dup activities and therefore seldom used.

OPERATOR VERIFICATION OF DATA ON TAPE

1. The operator causes data on the tape record to be read into the memory unit.

2. Data from the source document is rekeyed and compared against data in the memory unit one character at a time. If the comparisons are equal the process continues.

3. If the comparisons yield an unequal condition, or a character of data in memory is not the same as its equivalent on the source document, the operator depresses the appropriate function keys. The operator then keys the correct character into the memory unit. The corrected character written on tape is read and compared automatically to the data stored in the memory unit.

Chapter 2

LEARNING THE KEYBOARD

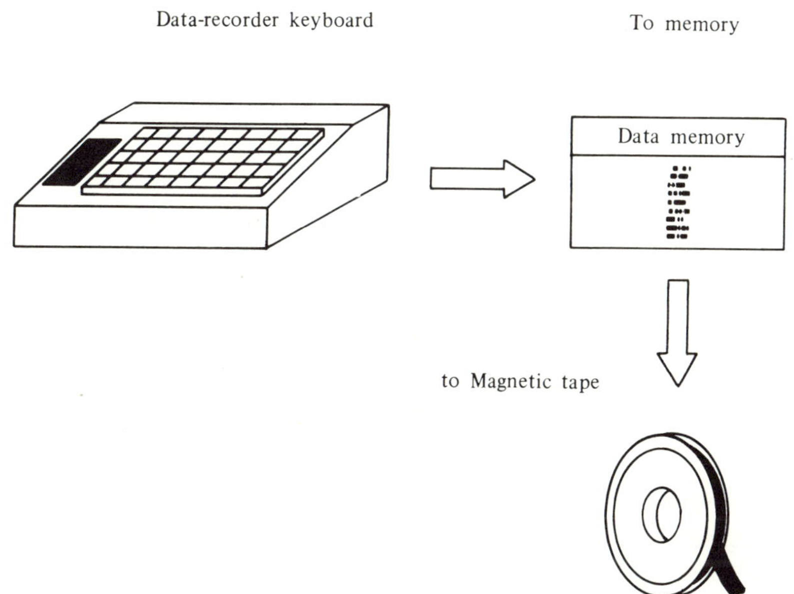

FIGURE 2-1

Data entered through the keyboard goes into the magnetic core memory unit before it is recorded on magnetic tape. On a typewriter, characters are recorded visually. Keypunched characters are punched into cards and may be seen as printed characters on top of a punched card. On the data recorder, however, characters are recorded on magnetic tape. They are not visible to the operator except through the display unit.

A typewritten page may contain several thousand characters, while a punched card can only contain 80 characters. A magnetic tape record in the basic data recorder may contain up to 100 characters. The information on an 80-column punched card can be reduced in size to less than one inch on magnetic tape as shown in Figure 2-2. The actual amount of space required by a complete 100-character record is shown in Figure 2-3.

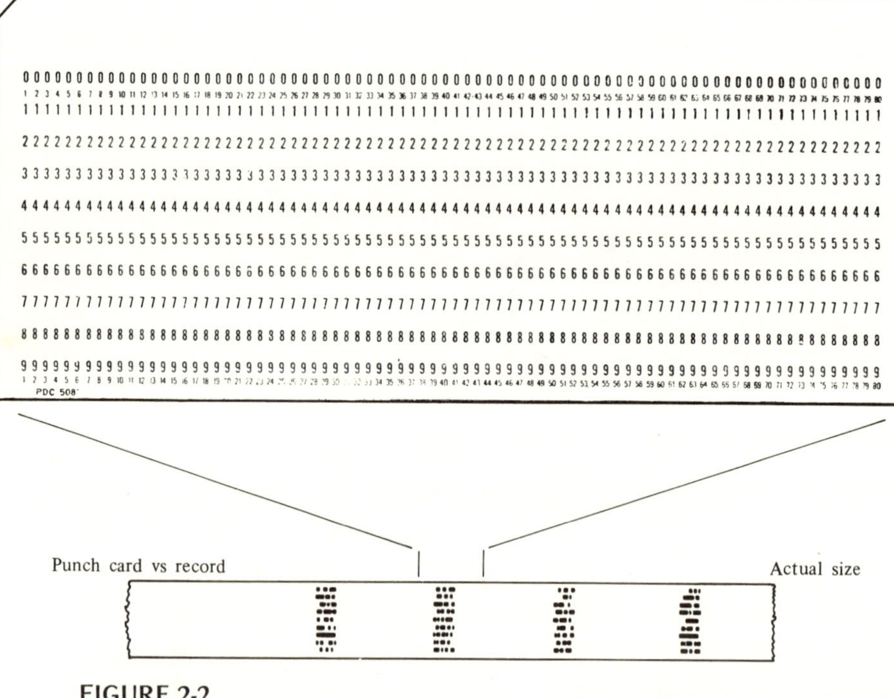

FIGURE 2-2

The keyboard of a data recorder is shown in Figure 2-4. Some of the keys are familiar to a typist and some are unique to

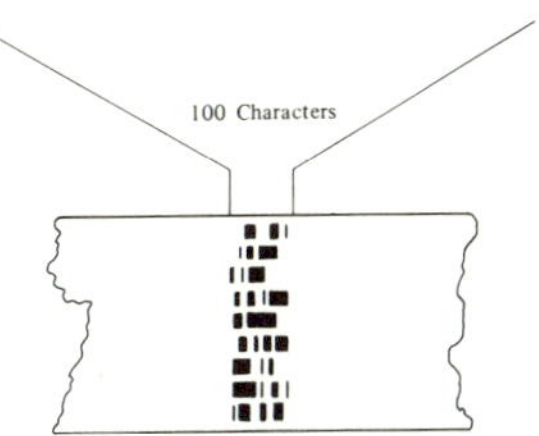

FIGURE 2-3

the data recorder. The keys on the data recorder are colored to
facilitate the machine operations. There are three white keys
(Figure 2-5) having only one character assigned to them. They
are: T, A, and Z. The *blue* keys contain all numeric characters
(0-9) the slash and minus (–) sign. The *white* keys contain all
other characters while the *red* keys are used as special control
keys and are discussed later on in the text.

Some keys, like typewriter and keypunch keys, are used for
two characters, one *upper* and one *lower*. The upper character

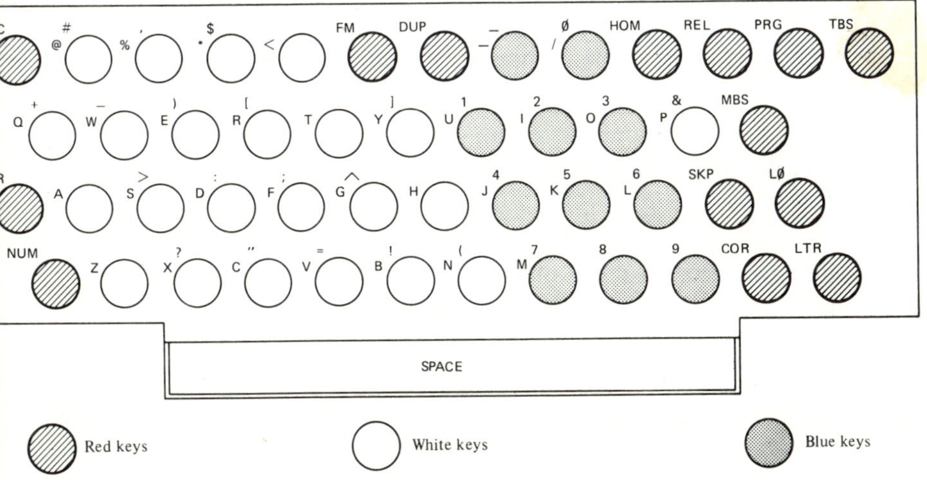

FIGURE 2-4

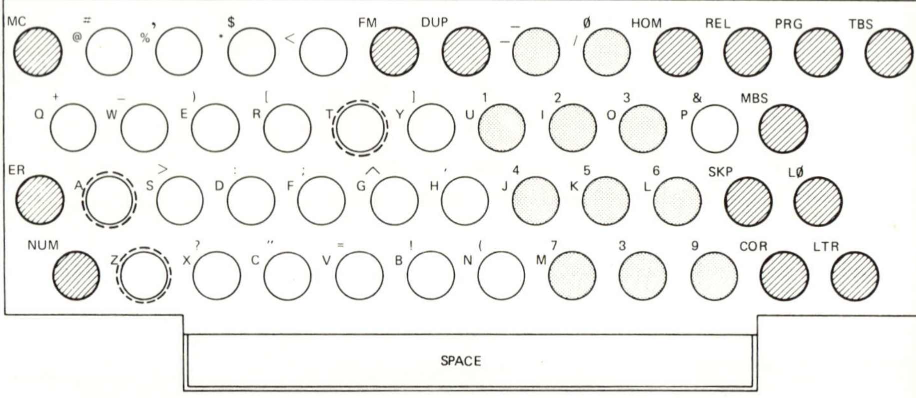

FIGURE 2-5

of the blue keys is a digit from 0 to 9 or a dash or minus sign.
The upper characters of the white keys are *special* characters.
As does the typewriter and the keypunch, the data recorder has
a space bar which represents a blank space.

All upper characters are referred to as numeric characters
even though they all do not represent digits. They contain:

$$0,1,2,3,4,5,6,7,8,9,\#,,,\$,.,+,-,',:,$$
$$[,],>,:,\wedge,?,",=,-,!,(,),\&$$

All lower characters are referred to as alphabetic or alpha
characters even though they do not all represent letters of the
alphabet. These are:

$$A,B,C,D,E,F,G,H,I,J,K,L,M,N,O,P,Q,R,S,\ T,U,V,W,X,Y,Z,$$
$$@,\%,*,<,-,/.$$

Note that the dash (-) and the space bar are *both* numeric and
alphabetic. All of the keys we have been discussing in this
section represent members of the data recorder *character set*.

At the center of the keyboard and directly over the keys is a
flat black plastic unit (Figure 2-6) divided into several sections
and labeled POSITION, CHAR, and PROG.

The section labeled CHAR is called the *MEMORY DISPLAY*.
It displays the contents of a single location in data memory.

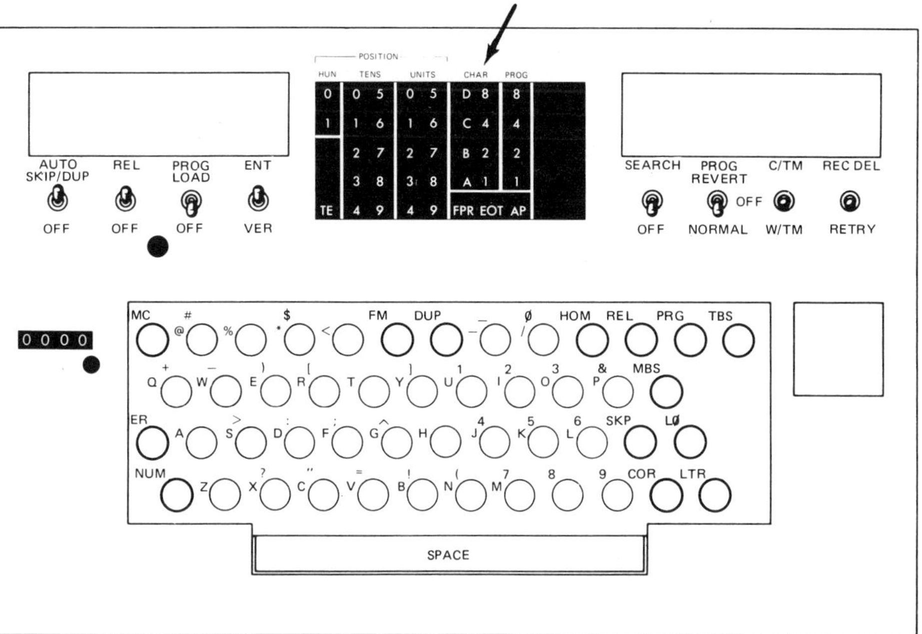

FIGURE 2-6

The specific location in the core memory is specified by the section labeled POSITION (The section labeled PROG refers to program codes and is discussed in Chapter 4.)

Look for CHAR on your keyboard.

In the CHAR section there are eight lamps labeled DCBA8421 (These have already been mentioned in Chap. 1). These lamps will light up in various combinations to represent a member of the data recorder character set.

CHAR

D	8
C	4
B	2
A	1

When the DCBA lamps are all ON then a digit or number is in the memory location under consideration. The number is

specified by the 8, 4, 2, 1 lamps.
The number 1 is represented as:

D
C
B
A   1

Two is represented as:

D
C
B   2
A

Three is represented as 2 + 1 or:

D
C
B   2
A   1

By referring to Table 1-1 and Table 2-1 we can see that the digits 0-9 can be represented in MEMORY DISPLAY (CHAR) as:

TABLE 2-1

0	DCBA	
1	DCBA	1
2	DCBA	2
3	DCBA	21
4	DCBA	4
5	DCBA	4 1
6	DCBA	42
7	DCBA	421
8	DCBA	8
9	DCBA	8 1

Note that: 3 = 2 + 1
5 = 4 + 1
6 = 4 + 2
7 = 4 + 2 + 1
9 = 8 + 1

and zero is specified with only the DCBA lamps ON.

Letters of the alphabet are represented in CHAR in a similar manner *except* that no letters begin with all four of the DCBA lamps ON at the same time. At least two lamps must be on however, to represent a letter. These lamps are DC.

A is represented as:

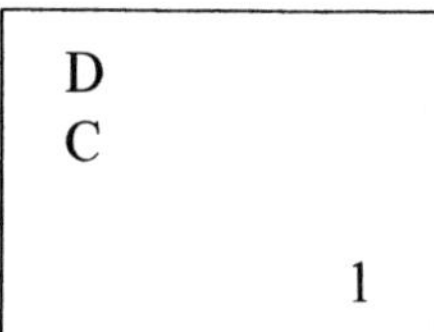

K is represented as:

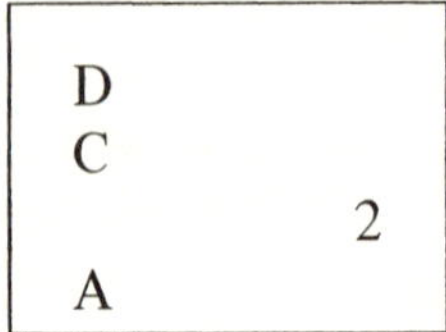

Z is represented as:

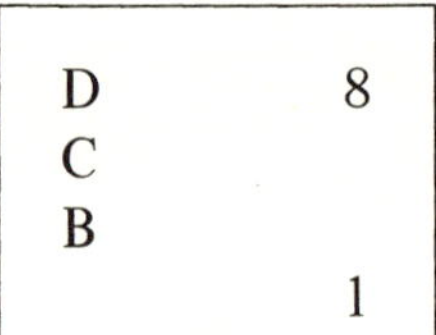

The code for representing letters is easy to learn. It is shown in Table 2-2.

There are horizontal lines between I and J, and R and S to indicate the pattern of coding. A through I are specified by lamps DC and corresponding numeric values 1-9. J-R are specified by lamps DCA and corresponding numeric values 1-9. S-Z are specified by lamps DCB and corresponding numeric values 2-9.

Sometimes it is easier to determine a particular letter by counting on your fingers. Thus, if DCA 8 appeared in CHAR you would first note that DCA referred to the letters J-R. Finger counting begins with J and Q is the eighth letter in this series.

Figure 2-7 contains the MEMORY DISPLAY codes for all of the characters in the data recorder character set. Note that in handwritten source documents much confusion occurs between the letter "oh" and the digit zero. A zero is an ellipse and should be slashed (∅), to avoid being read as the letter oh (O). There are other characters that can cause confusion and Table 2-3 illustrates how they may be specified when writing them by hand on source documents.

TABLE 2-2

Letter	Memory Display Code
A	DC 1
B	DC 2
C	DC 21
D	DC 4
E	DC 4 1
F	DC 42
G	DC 421
H	DC 8
I	DC 8 1
J	DC A 1
K	DC A 2
L	DC A 21
M	DC A 4
N	DC A 4 1
O	DC A 42
P	DC A 421
Q	DC A 8
R	DC A 8 1
S	DCB 2
T	DCB 21
U	DCB 4
V	DCB 4 1
W	DCB 42
X	DCB 421
Y	DCB 8
Z	DCB 8 1

TABLE 2-3

O	letter "O"	Ø	digit zero
I	letter "I"	1	digit one
Z̶	letter "Z"	2	digit two
V̶	letter "V"	U	letter U

A DC 1	H DC 8	O DC A 42	V DCB 4 1	2 DCBA 2	9 DCBA8 1	! C 8421	∧ C A8421	? CB 8421
B DC 2	I DC 8 1	P DC A 421	W DCB 42	3 DCBA 21	Sp C	& C A	−CB	: CBA8 2
C DC 21	J DC A 1	Q DC A8	X DCB 421	4 DCBA 4	] C 8 2	[C A8 2	/ CB 1	# CBA8 21
D DC 4	K DC A 2	R DC A8 1	Y DCB 8	5 DCBA 4 1	. C 8 21	$ C A8 21	, CB 8 21	@ CBA84
E DC 4 1	L DC A 21	S DCB 2	Z DCB 8 1	6 DCBA 42	< C 84	* C A84	% CB 84	' CBA84 1
F DC 42	M DC A 4	T DCB 21	Ø DCBA	7 DCBA 421	(C 84 1	) C A84 1	__CB 84 1	= CBA842
G DC 421	N DC A 4 1	U DCB 4	1 DCBA 1	8 DCBA8	+ C 842	; C A842	> CB 842	" CBA8421

FIGURE 2-7

OPERATING THE TAPE RECORDER

Fig. 2-8 shows the POWER switch. It is found on left side of the tape deck.

Fig. 2-9 shows the location of the ERROR LIGHT. Perform the following:

1) Turn the POWER switch ON.
   The flashing ERROR LIGHT will come ON.
2) Turn the POWER switch OFF.

Each time the POWER switch is turned on the ERROR LIGHT will start to flash. At this time the keyboard is locked or inoperative. Refer again to Fig. 2-9 and notice the ER key. If

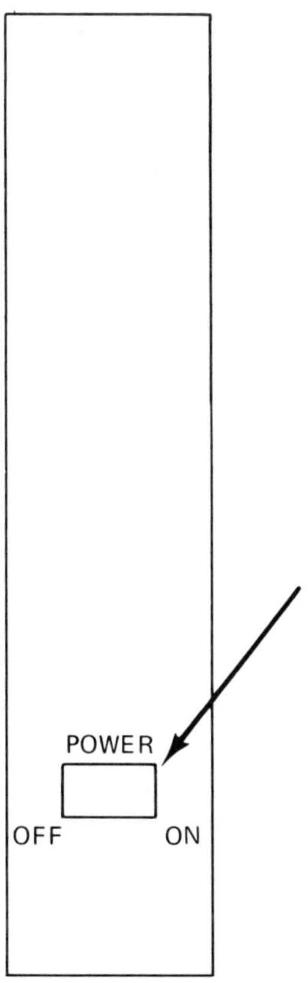

FIGURE 2-8

the ERROR LIGHT is on and the ER key is depressed, the ERROR LIGHT will go off.

Perform the following operations:

1)   Turn the POWER switch ON.
     The flashing ERROR LIGHT will come ON.
2)   Depress the ER key.
     The flashing ERROR LIGHT will go OFF.
3)   Turn the POWER switch OFF.

Perform the following operations:

1)   Turn the POWER switch ON.
2)   Press the ER key.
3)   Look at the POSITION DISPLAY lamps. (Fig. 2-10).
     They show 001. This specifies that you are in column 1.
4)   Turn the POWER switch OFF.

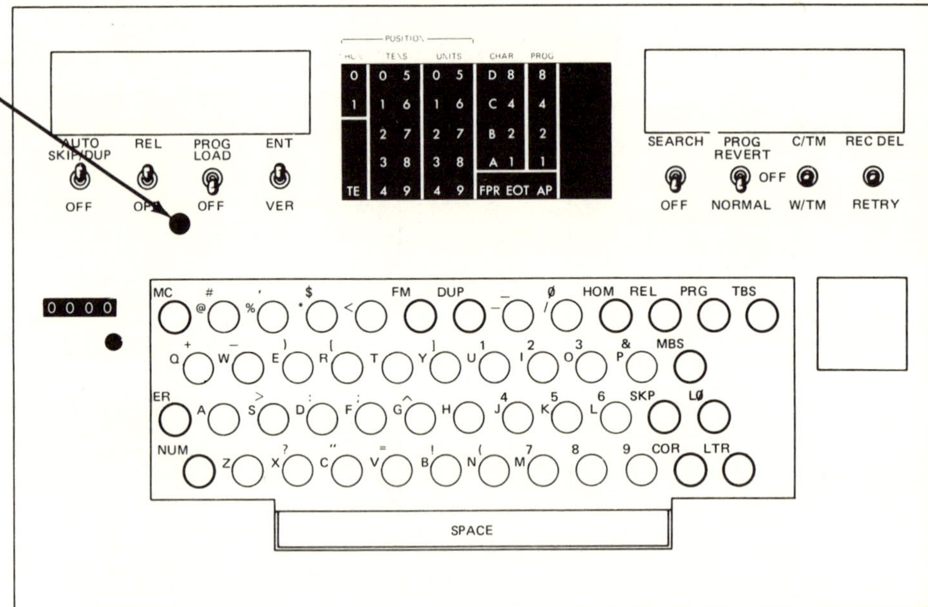

FIGURE 2-9

Position Display

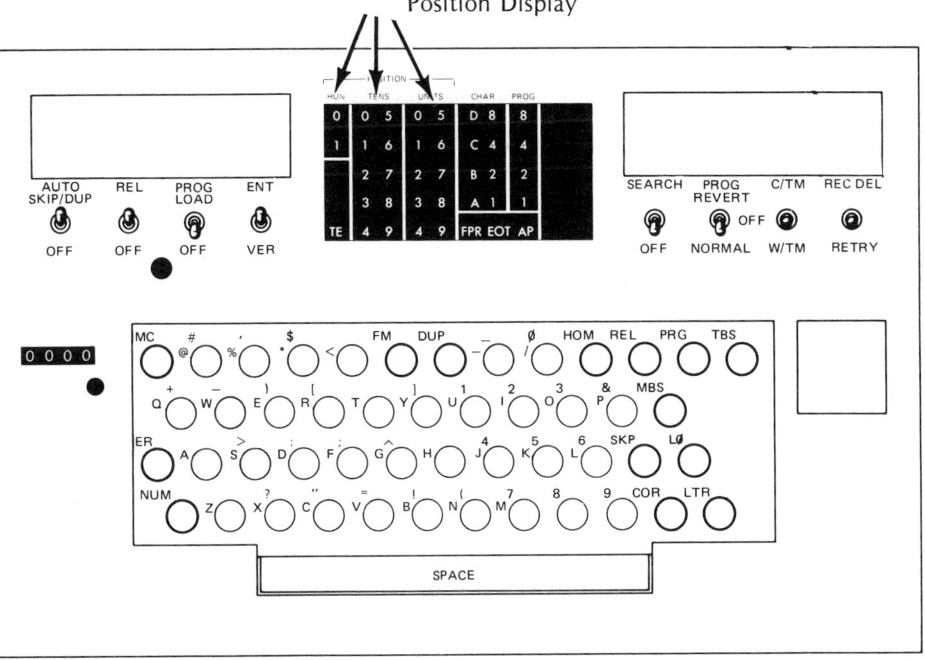

FIGURE 2-10

The POSITION DISPLAY lamps appear as:

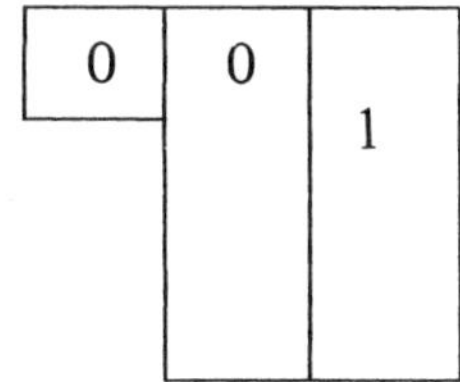

when specifying position 001.

The following examples show how to read the lamps in POSITION DISPLAY.

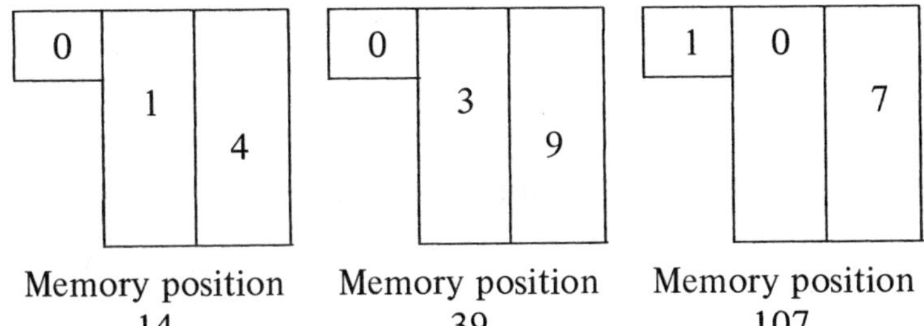

Memory position 14   Memory position 39   Memory position 107

Perform the following operations:

1) Turn the POWER switch ON.
   The memory position displayed is 001.
2) Depress the ER key.
3) Place the 4th control switch from the left in the ENT position.
4) Depress the space bar once by tapping it and releasing quickly.
   You have keyed a space or blank character into position 001. The POSITION DISPLAY is now at 002 and is ready to accept a character in this position.
5) Tap the space bar once more. You have keyed a blank character into location 002 and the POSITION DISPLAY is now at 003.
6) Turn the POWER switch OFF.

The MBS Key

The *Memory Backspace Key* or MBS allows you to "back-up" in memory much like the typewriter backspace key moves the carriage backwards.

The MBS key is a "protected" red colored key. To demonstrate what is meant by a "protected" key perform the following operations:

1) Turn POWER switch ON.
   Do not depress the ER key but place the 4th control switch from the left in the ENT position.
2) Tap the space bar several times.
   Note that POSITION DISPLAY does not change because the ER key was not depressed and the keyboard was inoperative.
3) Depress the ER key.
4) Tap the space bar five times.
   The POSITION DISPLAY should show memory position 006.
5) Depress the MBS key. The POSITION DISPLAY does not change.

6) *Hold down* the ER key and at the same time depress the MBS key and watch POSITION DISPLAY back up one position at a time.
7) Turn the POWER switch OFF.

To use the "protected" MBS key, you must also *hold down* the ER key: this prevents an error situation when the MBS key is depressed accidentally. In the remainder of this text we shall specify ER/MBS when using the MBS key.

Several of the red function keys are protected keys. They are:

> COR   Correction Key
>
> FM   Field Modify Key
>
> HOM   Home Key
>
> MBS   Memory Backspace Key
>
> TBS   Tape Backspace Key

When using protected keys, the ER key must also be held down. (When using blue or white keys the desired key is depressed.)
Perform the following operations:

1) POWER ON.
2) Depress the ER key.
3) Place the 4th control switch from the left in the ENT position.
4) Tap the space bar 9 times. The POSITION DISPLAY reads 010.
5) Depress ER/MBS 9 times.
   POSITION DISPLAY reads 001.
6) POWER OFF.

The HOM key

The home (HOM) key allows you to return to position 001 (or *home*) without the use of the ER/MBS keys. (The HOM key is also a protected key.)

Perform the following operations:
1) POWER ON.
2) ER.
3) Place the 4th control switch from the left in the ENT position.
4) Space to position 32.
5) Depress the ER/HOM keys. The POSITION DISPLAY shows 001.
6) POWER OFF.

For a practical application using the MBS key, perform the following operations:
1) POWER ON.
2) Depress the ER key.
3) Place the 4th control switch from the left in the ENT position.
4) Hold down the NUM key and enter the numbers 1234 (on the blue keys). Assume that position 003 should have a space instead of the numeric character 3.
5) Depress ER/MBS twice.
6) Tap the space bar once.
   You have now "erased" or taken away the 3 in memory position 3 and replaced it with a blank character.
   Memory positions 001 through 004 now contains 12 4.
7) POWER OFF.

The last exercise demonstrates the use of the ER/MBS keys in backspacing and error correction. For a practical application using the HOM key perform the following operations:
1) POWER ON.
2) Depress the ER key.
3) Place the 4th control switch from the left in the ENT position.
4) Hold down the LTR key and enter the letters ABCDEF. Assume that the letters should have been entered in reverse order. (FEDCBA).
5) Depress the ER/HOM keys.
6) Hold down the LTR key and enter the letters FEDCBA. The memory now contains the six letters in the correct sequence.
7) POWER OFF.

The last exercise demonstrates the use of the ER/HOM keys to return to memory position 001 to begin keying a record over. To correct a record you can alter any character in memory using the ER/MBS keys or the ER/HOM keys. The next exercise illustrates altering memory using the ER/HOM keys.

Perform the following operations:

1) POWER ON.
2) ER key.
3) Place the 4th control switch from the left in the ENT position.
4) Key an A into position 001.
5) ER/HOM keys.
6) Read MEMORY DISPLAY. It shows the letter A (DC   1).
7) Key a B into position 001.
8) ER/HOM keys.
9) Read MEMORY DISPLAY. It shows the letter B (DC   2).
10) Key a C into position 001.
11) ER/HOM keys.
12) Read MEMORY DISPLAY. It shows the letter C (DC   21).
13) POWER OFF.

REVIEW OF MEMORY DISPLAY AND MEMORY POSITIONS

The POSITION indicators show the memory position that you *are ready* to key into and the MEMORY DISPLAY shows the contents of that position. When you key a character into memory, it *replaces* the character that was formerly there. Two keyboard drills follow:

1) A numeric character drill

2) An alphabetic character drill

GO SLOWLY and try to develop ACCURACY. Do not try for speed right away. Speed can be developed through use of the drills found in Appendix A. When practicing for speed, be sure to refer to the Speed Table on page 145 to determine your output rates.

Numeric Drills

(80 characters per line or record)

1001 2001 3001 4001 5001 6001 7001 8001 9001 1009 1008 1007 1006 1005 1004 1003 1002 1001 1230 2340
2223 3334 4445 5556 6667 7778 8889 9990 0999 9888 8777 7666 6555 5444 4333 3222 2221 0111 1000 0000
2345 6789 9876 5432 1010 1111 2222 3333 4444 5555 6666 7777 8888 9999 0000 1111 1212 1313 1414 1515
1616 1717 1818 1919 1010 5789 4890 3456 9091 1357 7890 0191 4511 1759 9825 8474 9894 7623 4332 7883
9094 5339 0093 8034 0039 8779 3522 4730 0300 8330 3662 9288 2357 9985 6486 8332 9801 1171 9018 1541

8674 4883 0912 2916 7905 1441 3903 3182 2658 2870 0927 0007 8190 9651 4823 3652 9876 2976 9082 2981
4564 8984 4019 9833 3009 3811 1329 0990 7339 1186 0925 3480 8629 9472 9005 8704 9805 7590 1187 0751
5671 0916 1093 8971 8901 3591 1141 1231 1567 1661 1130 1129 9110 0071 6001 3461 1084 2087 0004 4192
9884 4782 2008 4658 8016 6910 4666 7864 4980 4926 6428 8762 2991 0589 5577 5588 4675 8901 1240 0048
9019 4000 5000 6000 7000 8000 9000 1000 2000 3000 4000 5000 6000 7000 8000 9000 8000 7000 6000 5000

Alphabetic Drill

(80 characters per line or record)

Roberts Austin Granger Ells Hawley Strohs Gillette Morgan Bohm Filler Geer Esten
Billiard Post Rowcliffe Black Dunlop Endicott Spitz Dorman Norton Newcomb Peters
Feldman Morris Lang Croff Alberts West Fairbanks Croldart Coffrann Kilner Wesley
VanDussen Mengs Werner Kent Goveia Gay Barnard Lockwood Mahoney Knight Evans Fay
Kraft Lacey LaBart Pierce Jeffreys Hunter Call Barone MacFarlin Kellogg Churchil
Carson Boldt Roblee Northrup Paladino Napp Mancuso Tumminello Woodward Wolfemann
Furgeson Raupp Correy Waite Fuller Henry Lapp Jones Keene Sweeney Parrish Tuttle
Whittaker Vanderwall Stoddard Ewell Underhill Sawyer Welch Carter Maynard Oliver
Kearns Francis Carr Taylor Welker Stringham Stone Krotz James Elmore Green Curke
Charles Dailey Bryne Almeter Harris Priolo Singer Dusen Klotzbach Gray King Koch

Chapter 3

USING THE MAGNETIC TAPE

KEEP THE DATA RECORDER AND TAPE CLEAN

Dust on tapes can cause reading or writing errors. Therefore, it is a good practice to clean the data recorder at the beginning of each day's operation. Instructions for cleaning are found inside the cover of the cleaning kit supplied by the manufacturer. The procedure is to first open the glass cover then:

1) Rewind the tape, if a tape reel is mounted.
2) Set the feed-rewind switch to LOAD and open the cover on the tape feed mechanism.
3) Moisten the cleaning strip using a solvent. (The cleaning strip and solvent are both found in the cleaning kit.)
4) Place the cleaning strip in the tape feed path. (See Figure 3-1)
5) Holding each end of the cleaning strip, move it back and forth several times.
6) Clean the READ/WRITE head, the erase head, and the swing rollers A and B with a solvent-moistened swab or patch.

7) Turn the **POWER** switch **ON**.
8) Use a dry patch of cleaning strip and wipe off excess solvent.
9) Hold the cleaning strip patch on each moving capstan to make certain that it is dry.

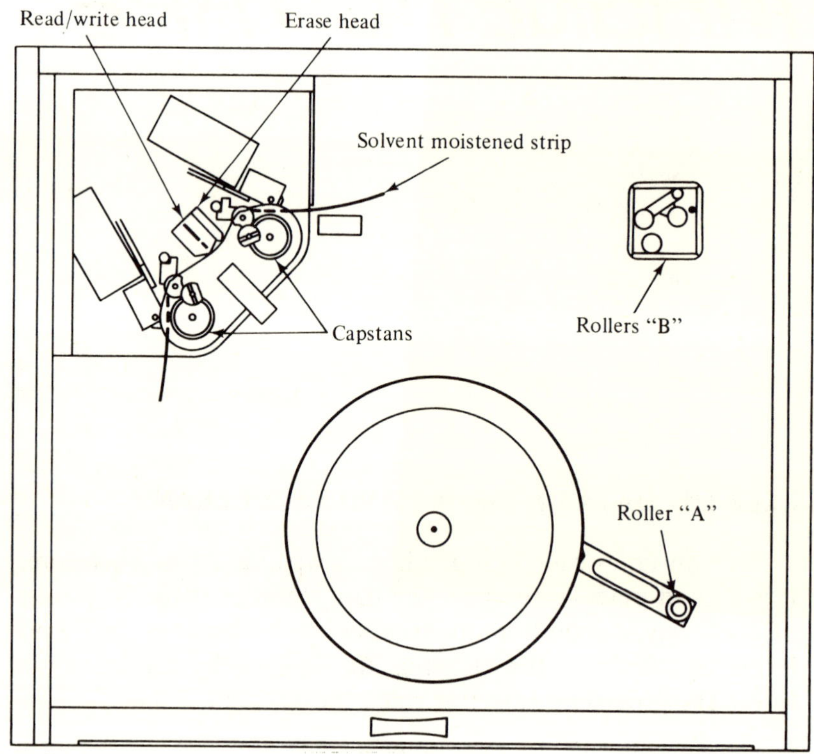

FIGURE 3-1

SWITCHES

Before you can enter a file of records onto magnetic tape, you must become familiar with the switches located above the keyboard.

FIGU...

Func... (Figure 3-2)

Wh... ing and duplicating is possib... switch: AS/D. When we want to turn th... switch ON we will write: SET SWITCH AS/D-ON.

Function of the RELEASE switch (Figure 3-3)

The RELEASE switch is shown in Fig. 3-3. When this switch is ON and the memory is filled, the contents of memory are written out on tape. When this switch is OFF you cannot write on tape. Its abbreviation is R. When we want you to turn this switch ON we will write: SET SWITCH R-REL

Function of the PROGRAM LOAD Switch (Figure 3-4)

When keying data from source documents, the PROGRAM LOAD switch must be off. This switch is abbreviated PL. When we want you to turn this switch ON we will write: SET

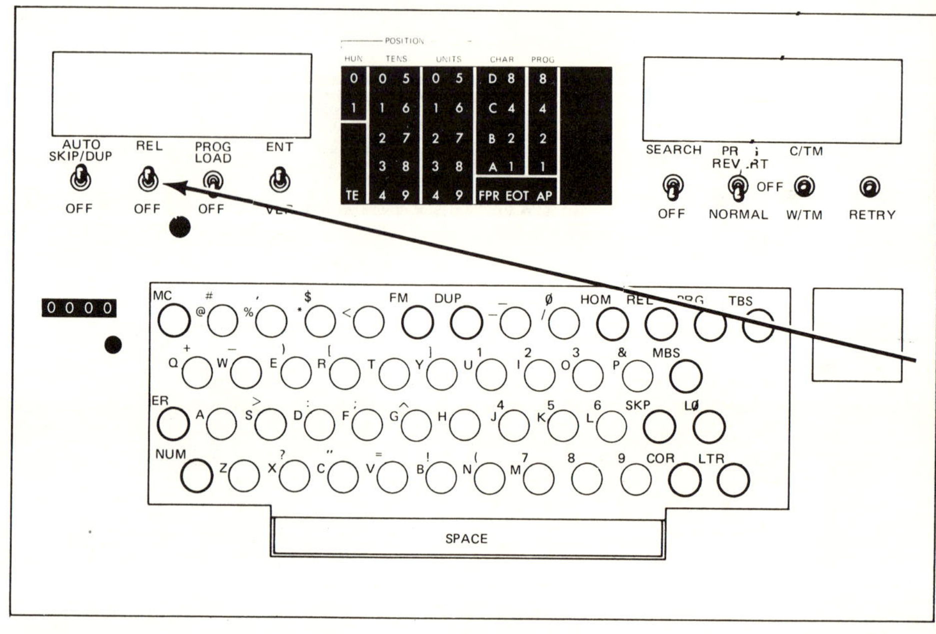

FIGURE 3-3

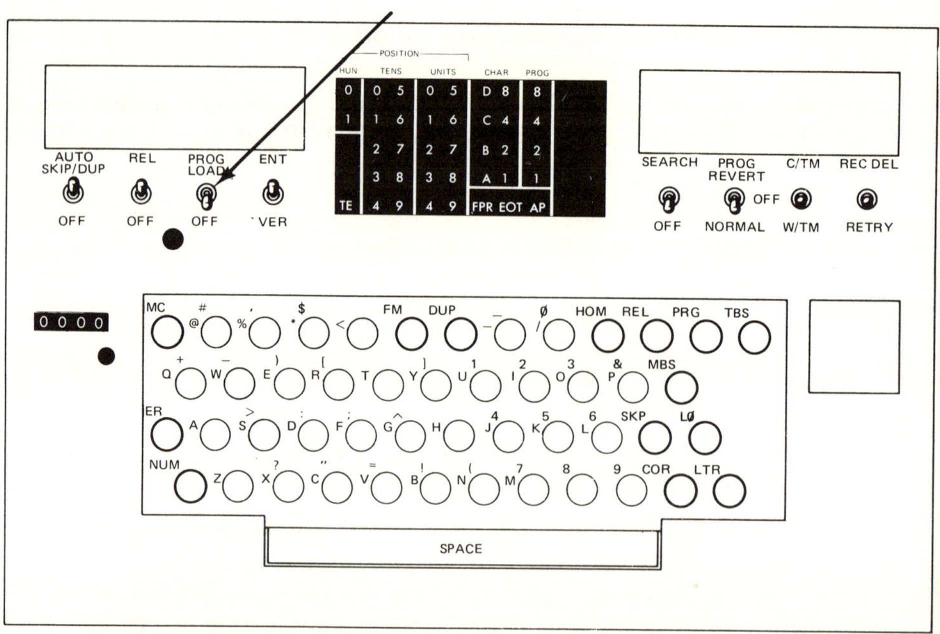

FIGURE 3-4

SWITCH PL-ON. (Preparing programs for the data recorder is discussed in Chapter 4)

Function of the MODE Switch

The MODE switch is shown in Figure 3-5. It is used to

1. Enter data into memory and
2. Verify data already in memory. Its abbreviation is M.

When you enter data you must set SWITCH M-ENT. When you are to verify data you must set SWITCH M-VER.

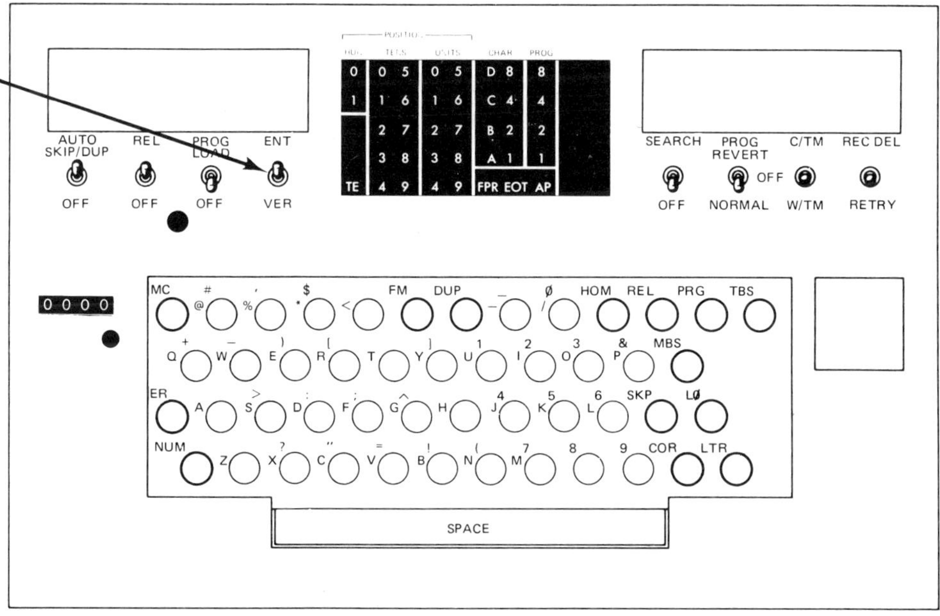

FIGURE 3-5

The next two function switches are not used in this section but their position is important. Therefore, you should know how to locate them to make sure the SEARCH switch is OFF and the program switch is set to NORMAL.

Function of the SEARCH Switch (Figure 3-6)

The SEARCH switch starts a search of a tape that contains data. Its abbreviation is S. When we want you to turn this switch OFF, we will write: SET SWITCH S-OFF.

Functions of the PROGRAM Switch (Figure 3-7)

(A three-position switch)

1. When this switch is in the OFF position, program codes cannot control the machine.

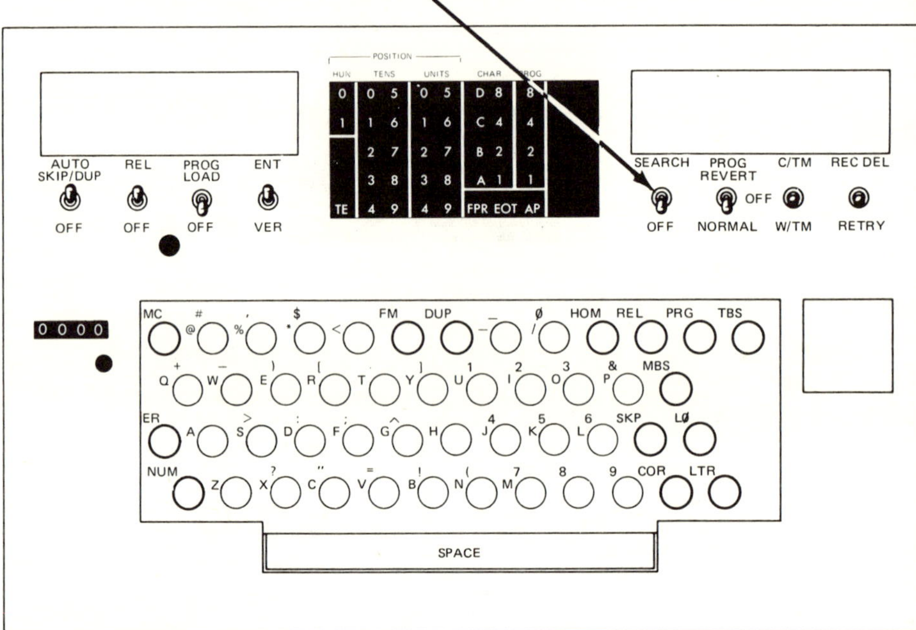

FIGURE 3-6

2. When this switch is in the REVERT position the data recorder automatically changes from alternate program control to main program control after a record is written on tape.

3. When this switch is in the NORMAL position the data recorder is under control of the program codes in either alternate or main program memory.

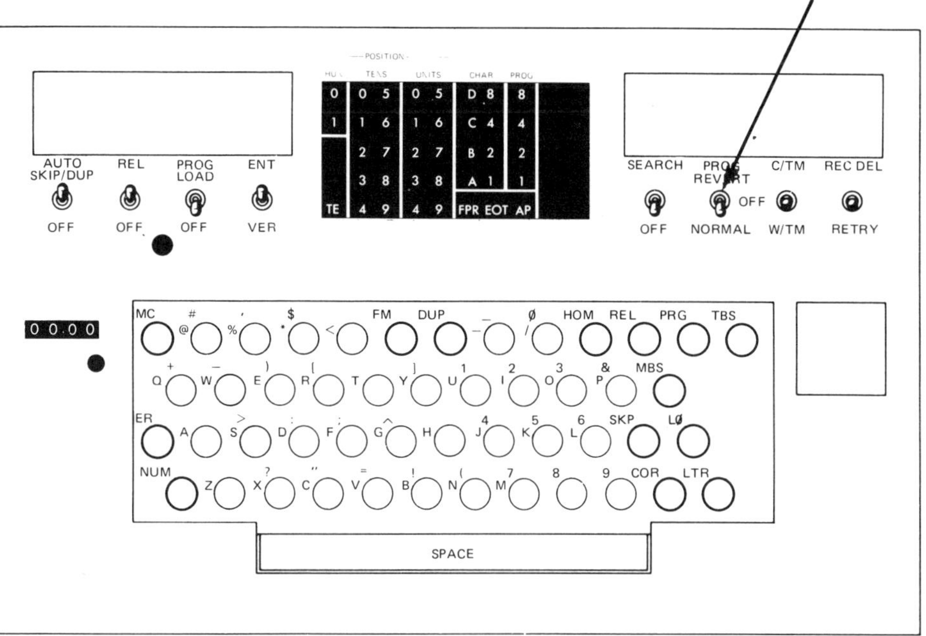

FIGURE 3-7

This switch is abbreviated P. When we want you to set the switch to the normal position, we shall write: SET SWITCH P-NORMAL.

LOADING THE TAPE

Look at the back of the tape reel and locate the plastic ring. If the ring is on the reel, you are able to write on the tape. When the ring is removed, you are unable to write on the tape. Remember the saying "No ring, no write".

Open the glass door on the tape deck by sliding it down. The back of the reel (containing the ring) must be placed against the tape deck. (See Figure 3-8.)

Next place the tape reel over the hub as shown in Figure 3-8 so that the tape will be coming off the right side of the reel. Then apply pressure against the reel with both hands, and push

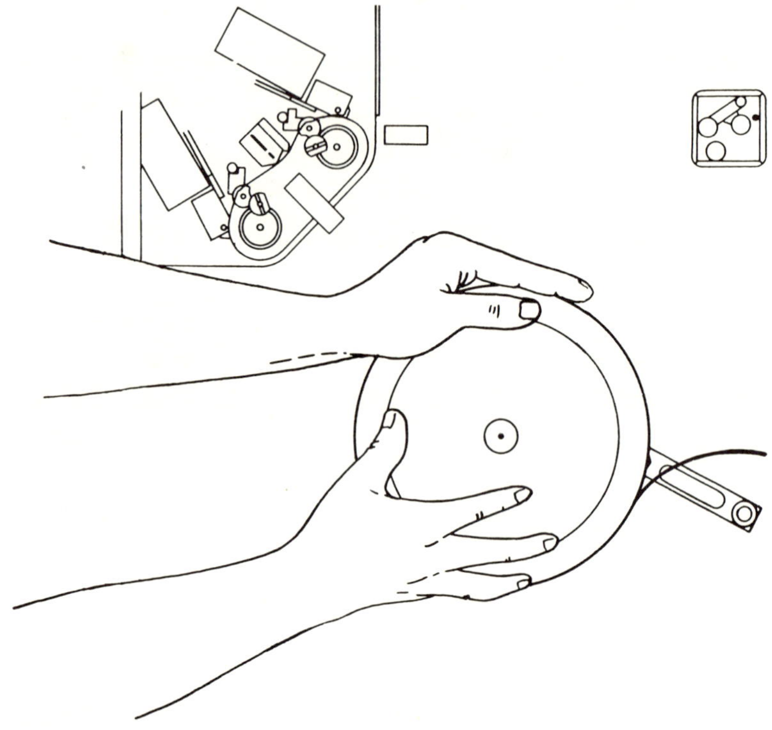

FIGURE 3-8

in firmly to snap lock the reel into place. The swing roller must be in the position shown in Figure 3-9. If it is not, move it up and to the left. Set the POWER switch ON.

Unwind about two feet of tape and set the FEED-REWIND switch to *LOAD*. The error light will begin to flash. DO NOT depress ER.

Open the door which covers the tape feed unit by lifting it up.

Thread the tape as shown in Figure 3-9. Set the FEED-REWIND switch to *FEED*, holding it in this position while the tape moves forward. Hold this switch until the tape stops. When the tape stops you will notice a reflective marker on the tape. The reflective marker should be positioned before the Read/Write and Erase Head. Release the FEED-REWIND switch. It should return to the *OPERATE* position. Depress the ER key to stop the ER light from flashing. Now that the tape is mounted, close the tape deck cover.

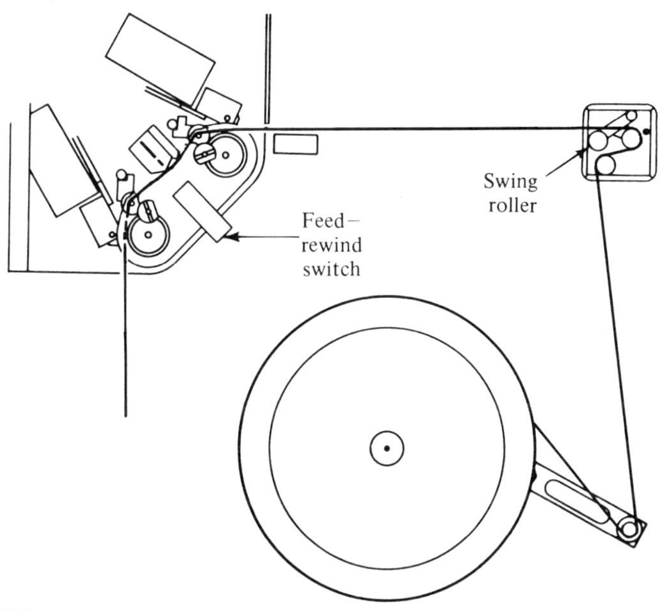

FIGURE 3-9

SET SWITCHES

AS/D — ON
R — REL
PL — OFF
M — ENT
S — OFF
P — NORMAL

The data recorder is now ready to accept data from the keyboard and enter it on tape.

Note: When the MODE switch is set M-ENT, the ring must be *on* the back of the reel. When the MODE switch is set to M-VER, the ring must be removed.

REWINDING THE TAPE

After a file of records has been written on magnetic tape, the reel must be rewound and removed. To do this, perform the following operations:

1) POWER-OFF and open the glass cover on the tape deck.
2) Remove the tape from roller A as shown in Figure 3-10.
3) Set the moveable roller to the rewind position as shown in Figure 3-11.

To avoid damaging the writing surface of the tape, do not use fingertips and fingernails on the tape. Use the side of your forefingers to move the tape.

4) Take up the slack in the tape by turning the reel counterclockwise on the hub.
5) Set the FEED-REWIND switch to *REWIND*. After a five second pause the tape will rewind. When the tape is

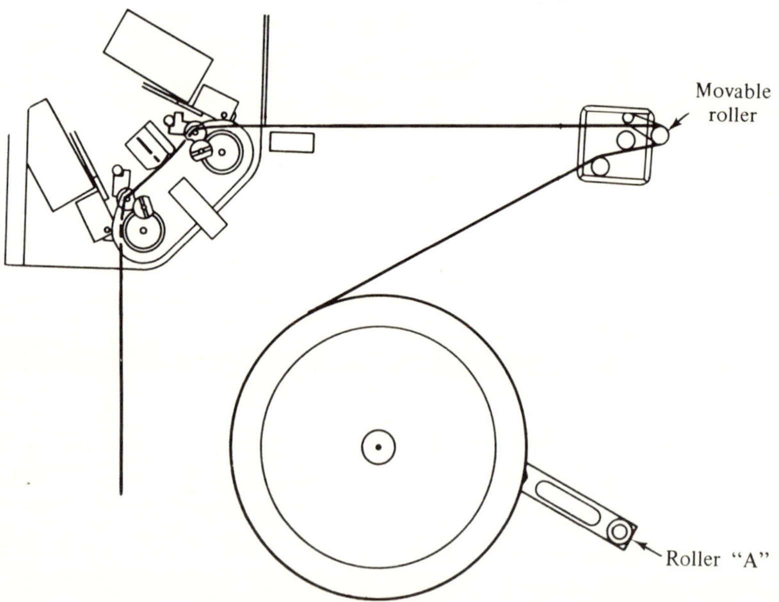

FIGURE 3-10

completely rewound, set the FEED-REWIND switch to *OPERATE*. Do not move this switch until the tape is completely rewound.

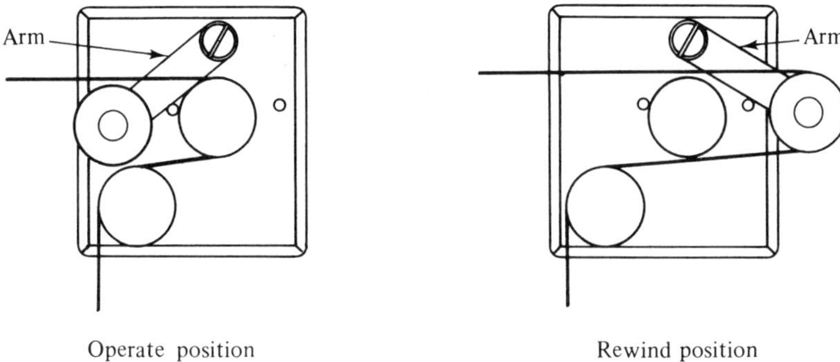

FIGURE 3-11

REMOVING THE TAPE REEL

To remove a reel of tape, grasp the reel firmly on two opposite sides. Press against the center of the hub with your thumbs and pull the reel outward. Close the glass cover on the tape deck.

Chapter 4

PROGRAMMING THE DATA RECORDER

The data recorder can be programmed to enter data in specified columns. In a similar manner the typewriter uses tab controls for margins and columns (or fields).

The data recorder operator enters a preset program containing the specified fields into the *program memory*. The program memory has the same number of positions as the data memory. For example, if the data memory contains 100 positions, the program memory also contains 100 positions. Once a program has been loaded into the program memory it remains there until replaced by a new program.

If a field is programmed for alphabetic characters, *any* alphabetic character may be entered by simply depressing the alphabetic character key desired. If a field is programmed for numeric characters, any digit (0-9) may be entered by depressing the numeric character desired.

At times it is necessary to enter numeric characters into alphabetic fields or alphabetic characters into numeric fields. If you wish to enter a numeric character into a field programmed as alphabetic, you must perform the following operations:

1) Depress and hold down the NUM key.
2) Key in the numeric character.
3) Release the NUM key.

If you wish to enter an alphabetic character into a field programmed as numeric, you must perform the following operations:

1) Depress and hold down the LTR key.
2) Key in the alphabetic character.
3) Release the LTR key.

Example 1:
Enter a T (an alphabetic symbol) into a programmed numeric field.

1) Depress and hold down the LTR key.
2) Depress the T key.
3) Release the LTR key.

If you do not depress the LTR key the error light will go ON when you depress the T key.

Example 2:
Enter a 1 (a numeric symbol) into a programmed alphabetic field.

1) Depress and hold down the NUM key.
2) Depress the 1 key.
3) Release the NUM key.

If you do not depress the NUM key the error light will go ON when you depress the 1 key.

Numeric fields typically take digits, the minus sign, or spaces. If you desire any other character (letter or symbol) you must depress the LTR key at the same time as you depress the other key for alphabetic lower case or the NUM key for upper case special characters.

The data recorder is designed this way to reduce errors on magnetic tape. Consider the following:

In attempting to enter a 3 into a numeric field, the operator accidently strikes the & (ampersand) key. The error light would come ON since the data recorder does not recognize the ampersand as one of twelve numeric characters. To recover from this error:

1.   Depress the ER key.
2.   Enter the 3.

Programmed Numeric Fields

When entering any digit (0-9) into a programmed numeric field it is only necessary to depress the desired number key. The NUM key (or numeric shift key) is not required. This rule also applies to the minus sign and the space key. Other numeric symbols (upper case characters) require the NUM key.

Programmed Alphabetic Fields

When entering any letter (A-Z) or any alphabetic symbol into a programmed alphabetic field, it is only necessary to depress the desired key. The LTR key (or alphabetic shift key) is not required. This rule also applies to the alphabetic symbols (lower case).

PROGRAM CODES

We noted earlier that fields may be:

1.   Alphabetic
2.   Numeric

3. Skipped   or
4. Duplicated

Each type of field is defined by unique program codes.

Programming Alphabetic Fields

To program an alphabetic field, key the digit 3 in the first position of the field and fill the remaining positions in the field with the digit 1. A six-position alphabetic field is programmed as 311111. The digit 3 defines the beginning of the alphabetic field. Five 1 digits are used for the remaining positions.

Programming Numeric Fields

To program a numeric field, key the digit 2 in the first position of the field. The remaining positions in the field are filled with spaces. Thus, a four-position numeric field is programmed as 2ƀƀƀ (ƀ means space). The digit 2 defines the beginning of the numeric field. The three spaces are used for the remaining positions.

Programming Skipped Fields

Often it is desirable to skip positions in a record or leave them blank. Blanks can be manually entered into a record by using the space bar; however, in large volume jobs this is time consuming and, therefore, costly. The unused positions can be skipped automatically by programming a skipped field. Key the digit 5 in the first position of the field. The remaining positions are filled with spaces.

A seven-position skipped field is programmed as 5ƀƀƀƀƀƀ. The digit 5 defines the beginning of the field. The remaining six positions are filled with spaces. Note that skipped fields may contain data.

Programming Duplicated Fields

Frequently such data items as date, social security number, employee number, etc., are required in consecutive records. Rather than keying in this information repeatedly, the data recorder can automatically duplicate this information. To program a data recorder to duplicate data in the same field from a previous record, the digit 4 must appear in the first *and* last position in the field. The positions between the two 4's are filled with spaces. A six-position field that contains duplicated information (alphabetic or numeric) is programmed 4ƀƀƀƀ4. The digit 4 defines the beginning and end of the field. The spaces are used for the remaining positions.

When using skipped or duplicated fields in entering data, the program in control must contain a 5 for skipped fields, or a 4 for duplicated fields *and* the AS/D function switch must be ON.

The data recorder displays the program code for the operator as shown in Fig. 4-1.

For example, if the field under consideration is a numeric field, lamp 2 will be lit in the column called PROG.

┌──────────┐
│   │
│   │
│   2 │
└──────────┘

If the field under consideration is a skipped field, lamps 4 and 1 (4 + 1 = 5) will be ON.

┌──────────┐
│   4   │
│   │
│   1   │
└──────────┘

After a program is loaded (See page 64) MEMORY DISPLAY shows the contents of the program memory as well as the data memory.

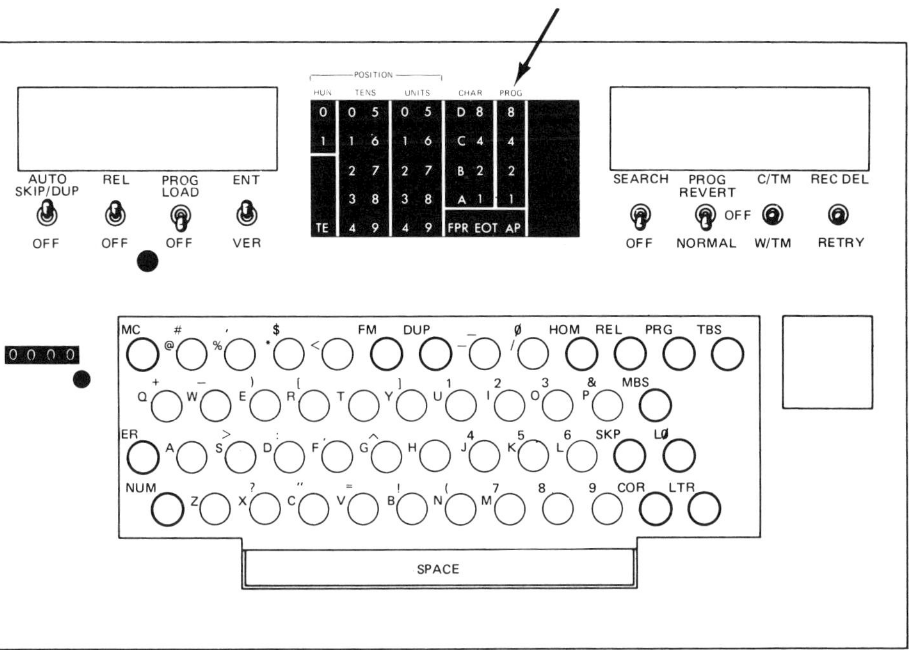

FIGURE 4-1

MAIN AND ALTERNATE PROGRAMS

It is possible to have two programs in the program memory, the MAIN or BASE program and the ALTERNATE program. Only *one* of these two programs can be in control at a time. The key which selects the MAIN or ALTERNATE program is located at the top right of the keyboard. (See Figure 4-2.)

The ability to use two programs is a time-saving feature. It is possible to enter two types of records on the same tape. Given records A and records B it is possible to key in a file of type A records then to continue on to a file of type B records without stopping to insert new program codes.

It is also possible to have two types of formats within one record. Assume a 100-character payroll record. The first 50 characters contain personal information such as social security number, name, and address. The second part of the record contains hours, rate, year-to-date totals for gross, net, union dues, FICA, state and federal taxes.

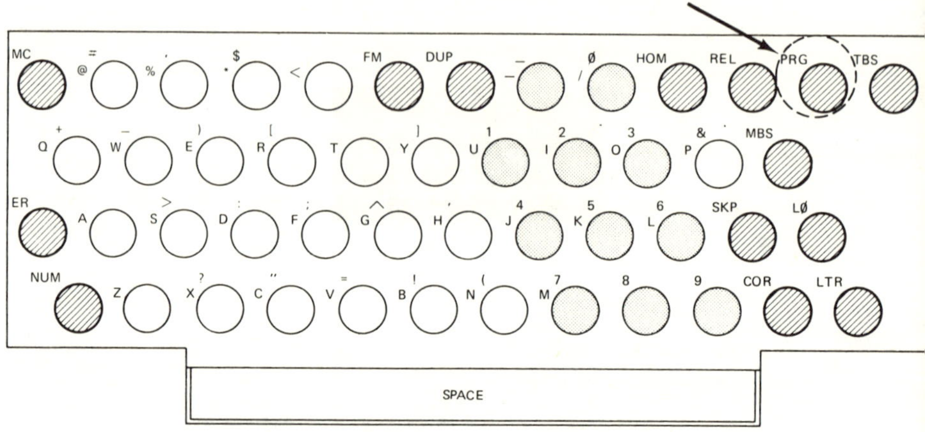

FIGURE 4-2

Each 50-character program is loaded into program memory
with the operator selecting the required program during the
keying operation.

If the program indicator lamps AP are OFF (See Figure 4-3)
the MAIN (or BASE) program is the controlling program, and
the PROG lamps refer to a MAIN program code.

If the program indicator shows AP (See Fig. 4-4), the
ALTERNATE program is the controlling program and the

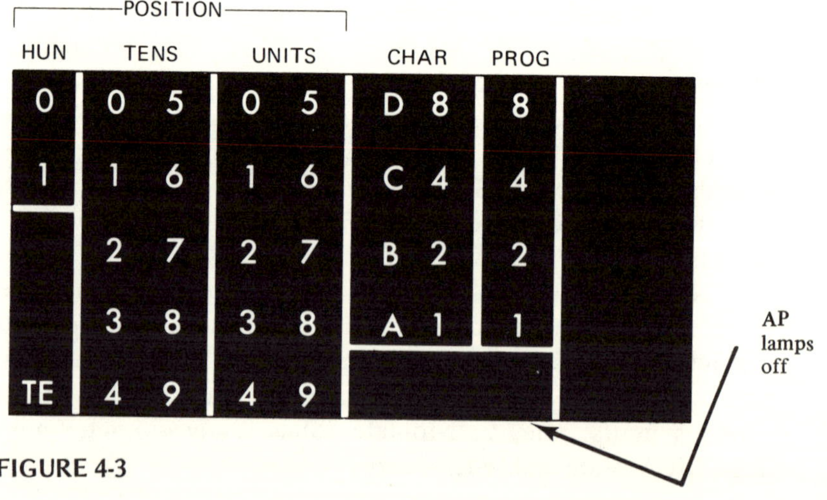

FIGURE 4-3

PROG lamps refer to an alternate program code.

By placing the data recorder under program control the operator can program the data recorder to change automatically:

From alphabetic shift to numeric shift

From numeric shift to alphabetic shift

To duplicate fields

To skip field

From alternate memory to main memory

From main memory to alternate memory

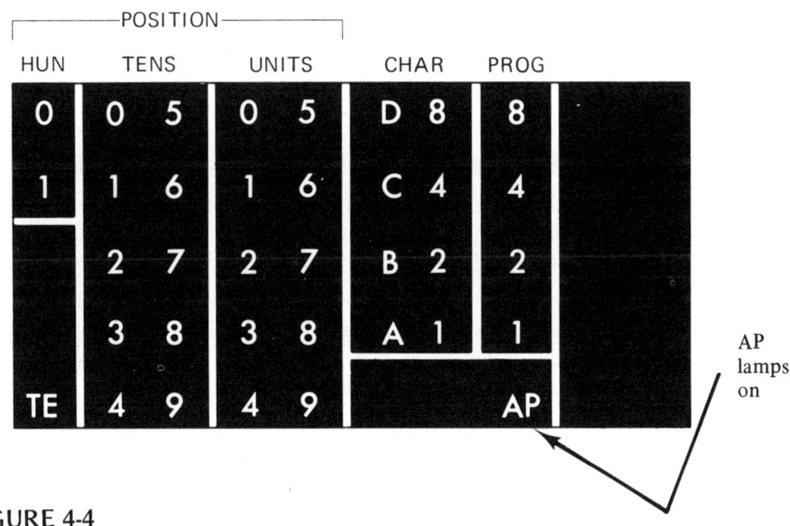

FIGURE 4-4

Perform the following operations:

1)   Set POWER switch ON.

2)   Depress the ER key.

3)   Look at the PROG lamps. Is MAIN or ALTERNATE program in control?
     (When POWER is turned ON, MAIN is usually controlling.)

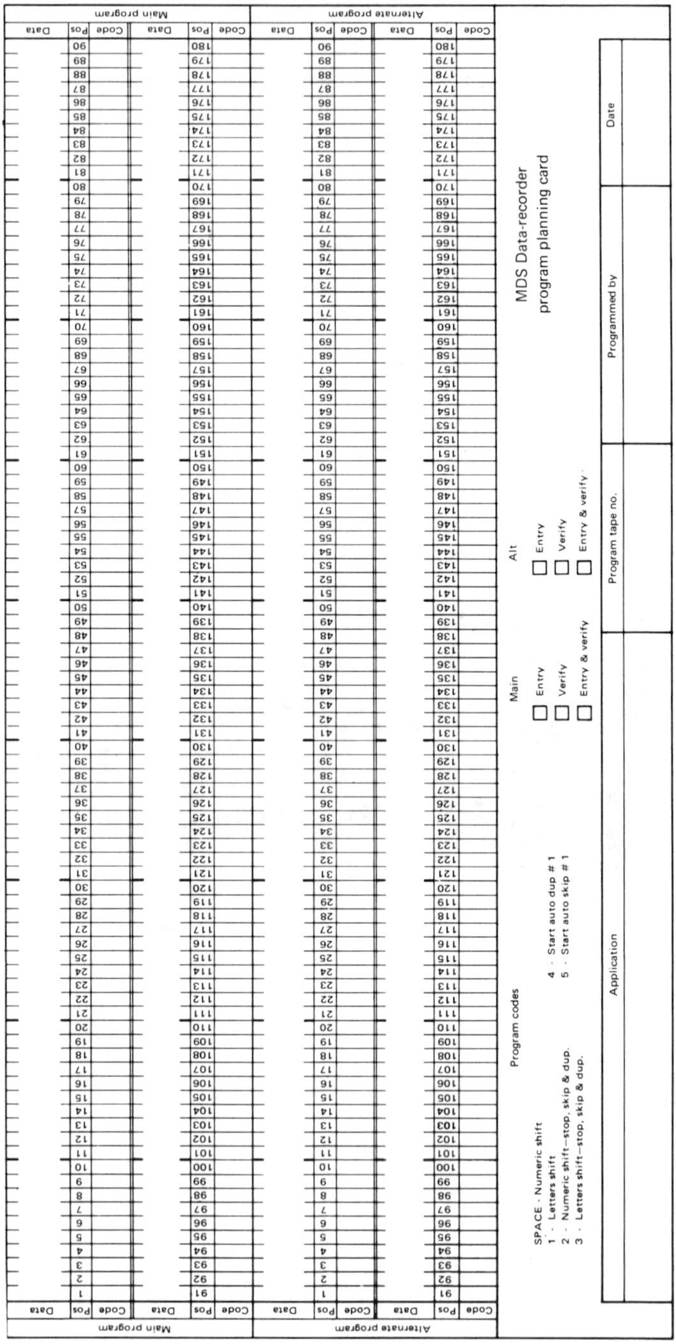

MDS Data-recorder
program planning card

Main program | Alternate program

Code | Pos | Data

Program codes

SPACE - Numeric shift
1 - Letters shift
2 - Numeric shift—stop, skip & dup.
3 - Letters shift—stop, skip & dup.
4 - Start auto dup # 1
5 - Start auto skip # 1

Main
☐ Entry
☐ Verify
☐ Entry & verify

Alt
☐ Entry
☐ Verify
☐ Entry & verify

Application | Program tape no. | Programmed by | Date

FIGURE 4-5

4) Depress the PRG key. The other program is in control. (Depress it again and the first program is in control.)

5) Turn POWER switch OFF

THE PROGRAM PLANNING CARD

The Program Planning Card (Fig. 4-5) assists the operator in planning and writing program codes. Note that there are sections for the MAIN and ALTERNATE programs.

In typical data entry jobs, many hundreds of documents are batched together and keying them to tape is expedited by presetting the data recorder to accept numeric information in some fields, alphabetic information in other fields, and skipping or duplicating other fields as appropriate. The use of program codes saves time when compared to the slower method of shifting for numeric and alphabetic characters and counting out the duplicated or skipped columns.

The Program Planning Card is used to describe fields and specify program codes.

Using Program Planning Cards saves time in keying records to tape. Consider the source document in Figure 4-6a. We could

XYZ Mfg. Co.   Billing date: 1/31/73

List of accounts receivable

Customer name	Address	Balance due
Towne Botique	32 Main St., Cleveland, Ohio	78.25
Tres Chic	92 Main St., Batavia, N.Y.	150.00
Sibleys	Main St., Rochester, N.Y.	200.00
Village Dept. Store	North Street, Lowell, Ill.	67.50
Bradners	River Street, Olean, N.Y.	175.00
McCurdys	Towne Dr., Rochester, N.Y.	200.00
Fashion Botique	55 Main St., Normal, Ill.	35.50
Helens Ski Haus	14 Pine St., Wilmington, Vt.	55.00
Karens Knit Wear	77 Main St., Lansing, Mich.	150.00
C.L. Carr Co.	113 Main St., Batavia, N.Y.	130.00

FIGURE 4-6a

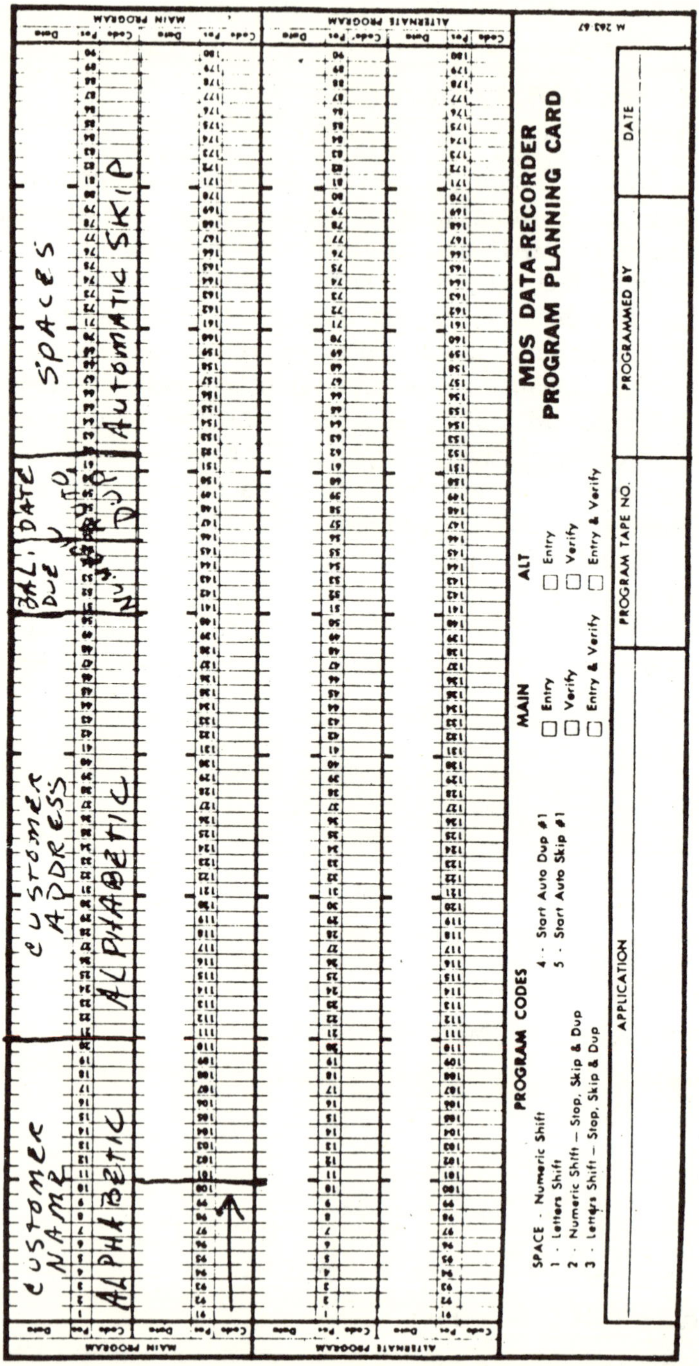

FIGURE 4-6b

describe the fields on the source document in Figure 4-6 on the following Program Planning Card (Figure 4-6b):

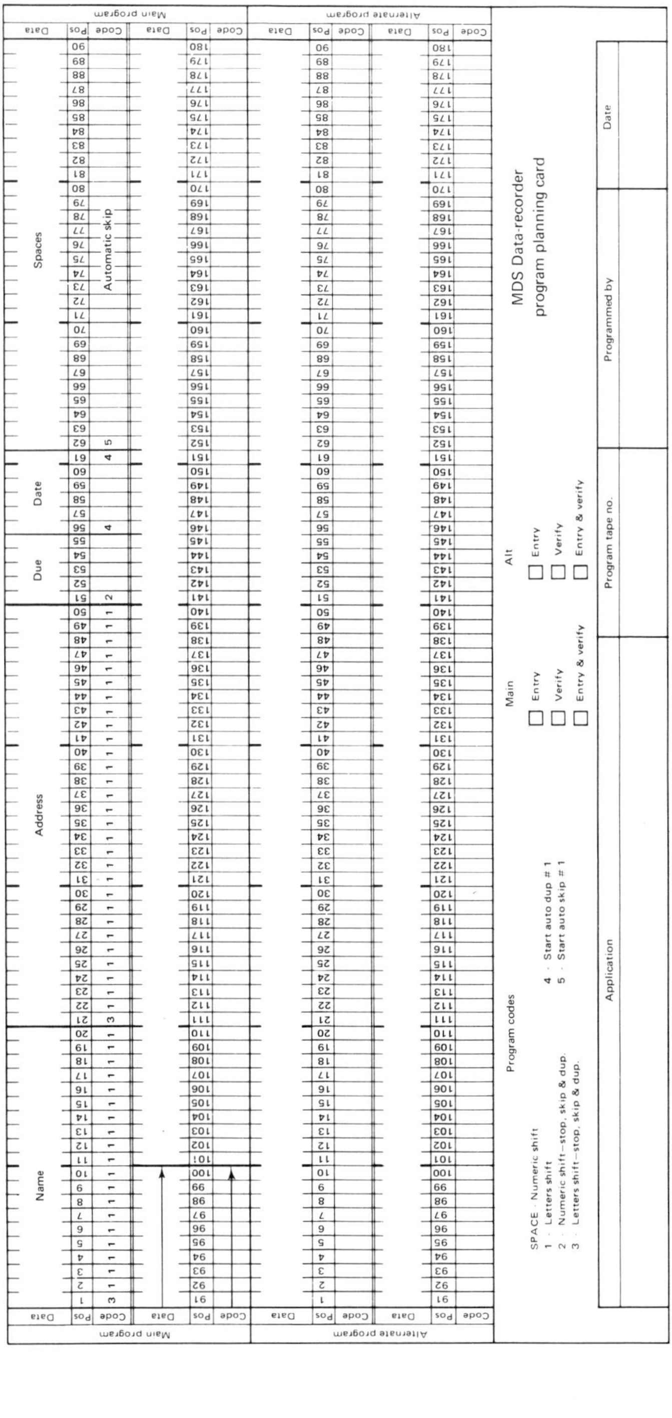

FIGURE 4-7

In Figure 4-7 the:

1)   Customer name is an alphabetic field 20 positions long.

2)   Customer address is an alphabetic field 30 positions long.

3)   Balance due is a numeric field five positions long (without the decimal point).

4)   Date is the billing date to be entered as a 6-position auto-dup field in each customer's record. (Without the slashes or/.)

5)   The remaining 39 positions are an auto-skip field with spaces.

The Program Planning Card contains 180 positions to accommodate the largest possible memory available on the data recorder. We use the number of positions appropriate for the record size and the following format to key the accounts receivable record from Figure 4-6a.

Record Positions	*Field Name*	*Data Type*
1 - 20	Customer Name	Alphabetic
21 - 50	Customer Address	Alphabetic
51 - 55	Amount Due	Numeric
56 - 61	Billing Date	Numeric/Duplicate
62 - 100	Spaces	Automatic Skip

First define the positions by drawing vertical lines. Second, name the fields. Now, fill in the appropriate program codes as shown in Figure 4-8.

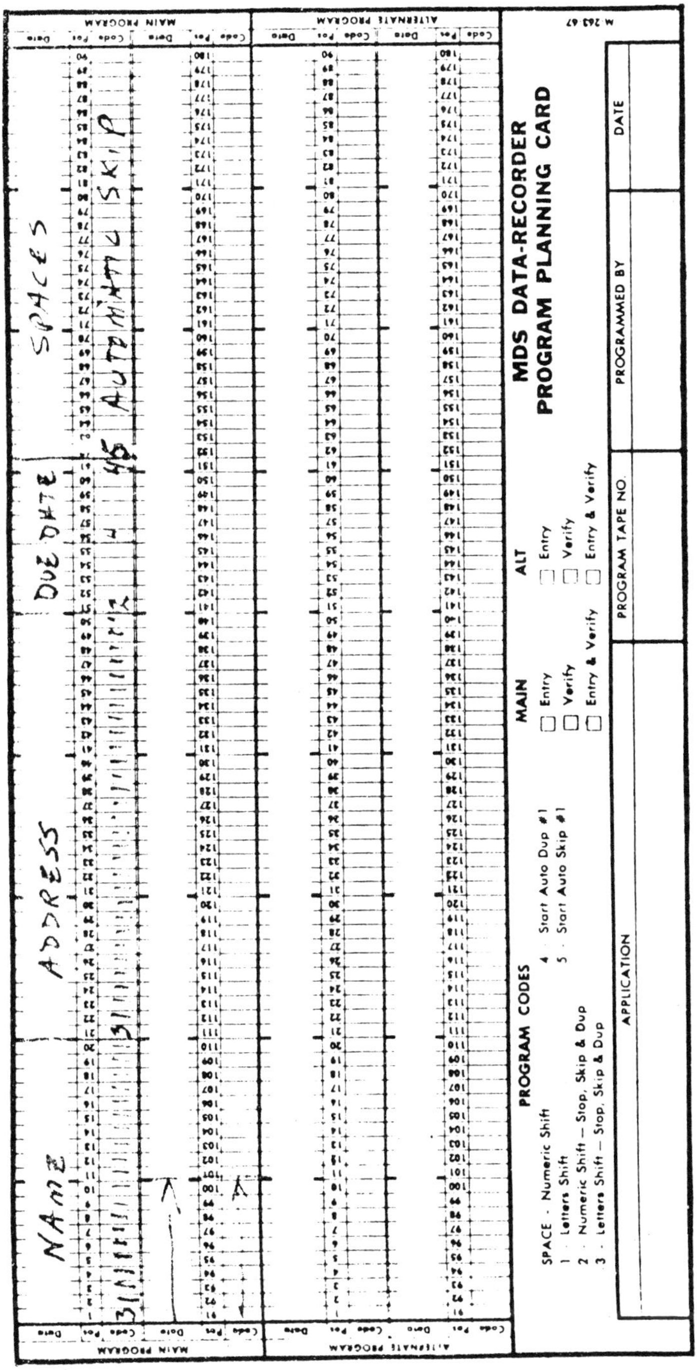

FIGURE 4-8

EXERCISES

*Prepare program cards for the following. (Each exercise requires 100 positions).

1. Record Positions	Field Name	Data Type
1 - 20	name	alphabetic
21 - 35	street	alphabetic
36 - 50	city and state	alphabetic
51 - 60	unused	automatic skip
61 - 66	purchase amount	numeric
67 - 100	unused	automatic skip

2. Record Positions	Field Name	Data Type
1 - 9	Social security no.	numeric
10 - 30	name	alphabetic
31 - 34	hours	numeric
35 - 40	unused	automatic skip
41 - 44	rate of pay	numeric
45 - 50	unused	automatic skip
51 - 56	date	automatic dup
57 - 58	dependents	numeric
59 - 100	unused	automatic skip

3. Record Positions	Field Name	Data Type
1 - 5	account number	numeric
6 - 25	customer name	alphabetic
26 - 40	customer address	alphabetic
41 - 48	date of last payment	numeric
49 - 60	unused	automatic skip
61 - 66	balance due	numeric
67 - 80	unused	automatic skip
81 - 88	billing date	numeric
89 - 99	unused	automatic skip
100 - 100	credit code	alphabetic

(Note that a field may be only 1 position in length as in credit code above.)

*Program cards are available from the vendor or at end of this text.

LOADING THE PROGRAM

Refer to the keyboard of your data recorder. It probably contains a device to alter the size of records. This device is shown in Fig. 4-9.

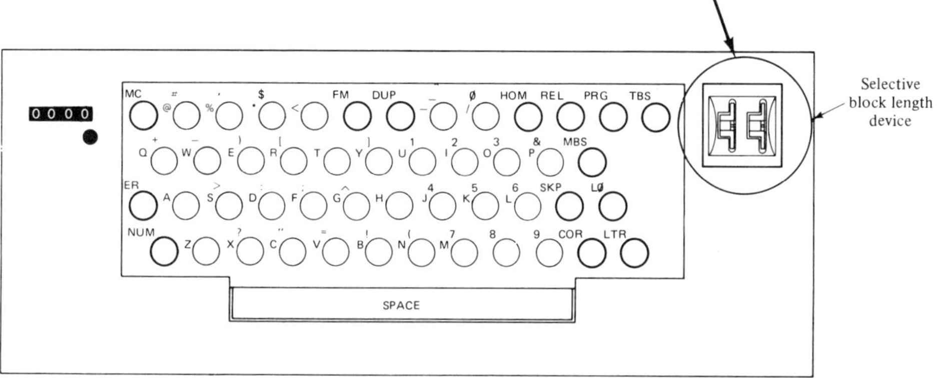

FIGURE 4-9

This device is called the Selective Block Length Device. It permits the operator to write in variable record lengths by "dialing" appropriate numbers. The following illustrates several settings for the Selective Block Length Device:

Dial Reading	*Number of Characters in Record*
18	180
16	160
13	130
08	80
05	50
03	30
01	10

Note that any desired record length equals the reading on the dial times 10. For example, to create a record length of 80, set the dial to 08. Then 08 x 10 = 80 (The desired number of characters in a record must always be in multiples of 10).

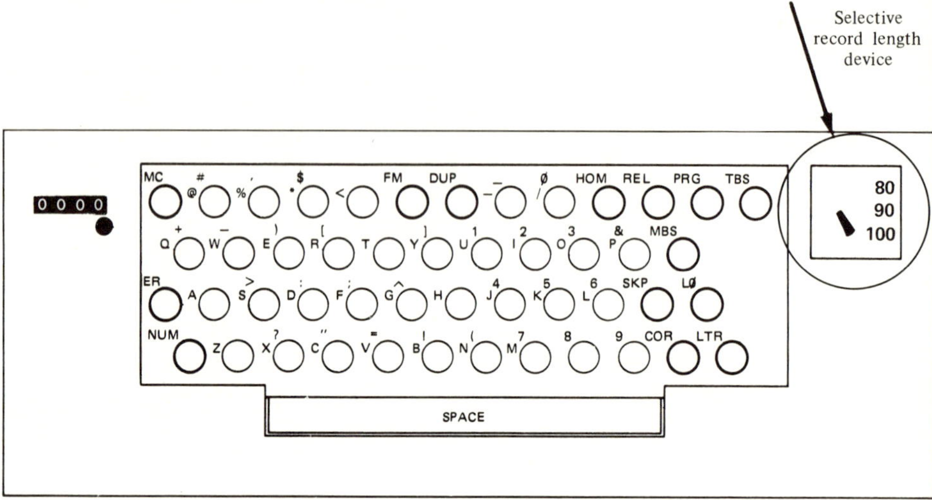

FIGURE 4-10

If your data recorder does not include the Selective Block Length Device it may include *The Selective Record Length Device* which permits the operator to write in 3 different record sizes:

an   80 position record

a   90 position record

a   100 position record

The desired record size is selected by moving the indicator to the appropriate number. (See Figure 4-10)

The next exercise requires you to load the program from exercise 1 into program memory. If your data recorder has only 80 positions available in memory, change the last field on the program card to read:

Record Positions	*Field Name*	*Data Type*
67 - 80	unused	automatic skip

LOADING YOUR PROGRAM THROUGH THE KEYBOARD

Using the Program Planning Card from Exercise 1, load the program into MAIN memory. Using the following instructions:

PROGRAM LOAD PROCEDURES

Instruction	*Explanation*
1. POWER ON	
2. SET SWITCH AS/D-OFF	to avoid duplication or skipping positions
3. SET SWITCH REL-OFF	to avoid writing on tape
4. SET SWITCH PL/PROG LOAD	to permit entry into program memory
5. SET SWITCH M-ENTRY	to write into memory.
6. SET SWITCH S-OFF	This switch is only used for searching.
7. SET SWITCH P-NORMAL	recommended position
8. Depress the ER/HOM keys	to begin at position 001
9. Depress the PRG key	to select the MAIN program
10. Hold down the NUM key and enter the entire program. You must depress a key for each position in memory. (Use the space bar for spaces)	to key in the program

VERIFICATION

11. CHANGE SWITCH M-VERIFY	to allow key verification
12. Depress the ER/HOM keys	to begin from position 001
13. Hold down the NUM key and key verify the entire program	to verify the entries made for program
If an error occurs the ER lamp will flash ON	
13a. Depress the ER key	to extinguish ER lamp
13b. SET SWITCH M-ENT	to permit entry of the correct character

13c. Key in the correct character

13d. Depress the ER/MBS keys — to back up to the error position

13e. Change SWITCH M-VERIFY — to permit verification of the corrected character

13f. Re-verify the corrected character and the remaining characters

14. Depress the ER/HOM keys — to return to position 001

15. CHANGE SWITCH PL-OFF — program loading has been completed

SIGHT-CHECKING PROGRAM CODES

Your program is now ready to control the data recorder for a data entry run. However, it is possible to examine each position in program memory to be certain that they contain the desired characters.

We can begin a new procedure after step 13f (omitting steps 14 and 15) by stepping backwards across memory positions using the ER/MBS keys.

Perform the following operations:

1) SET SWITCHES:

      AS/D — OFF
         R — OFF
       PL — OFF (with PL-OFF you cannot alter the program memory)
        M — ENT
         S — OFF
         P — NORMAL

2) Do not depress the ER/HOM keys to return to memory position 001.

    Remain at position 101, (or last position plus 1 in program memory). ER/MBS to position 100.

3) Compare the position in the program memory to the corresponding position on the program planning card for exercise 1 to verify that both positions contain the same characters.

4) ER/MBS to move to the next position.

Repeat steps 3 and 4 until you have displayed and compared all of the program memory to all the positions you entered on the program planning card.

The Multi-Code Key

Occasionally a character is required in memory and which can not be found in Fig. 2-7. These are called the *line feed* and 'idle' characters. The *line feed* character is B41. The 'idle' character is A421.

To enter these characters into memory you must use the MC or Multi-Code Key. Recall that the EBCDIC Code for the digit 4 is DCBA4. To key the digit 4 (using the MC key) into memory position 001, perform the following operations after depressing the ER/HOM keys:

SET SWITCHES

AS/D — OFF
REL — OFF
PL — OFF
M — ENT
S — OFF
P — NORMAL

1. Hold down the MC key

2. Key the letter D into memory

3. Key the letter C into memory

4. Key the letter B into memory

5. Key the letter A into memory

6. Depress the NUM key and key the number 4 into memory, this specifies the *second* digit in memory display which is the digit 4

7. Release the MC and the memory display advances to 002.

8. Depress the ER/HOM keys and memory position 001 will show

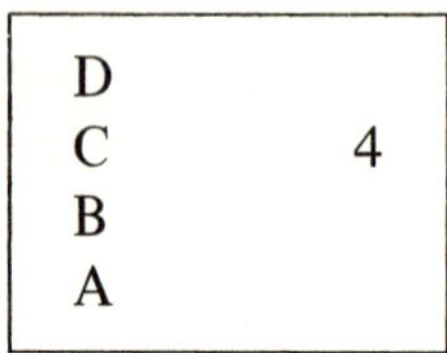

Exercise

Using the steps above to enter a 4 (in EBCDIC Code), enter a *line feed* character at memory position 021 and an *idle* character at memory position 025.

Chapter 5

DATA ENTRY

Entering data from source documents onto magnetic tape is sometimes called an *entry run*. Figure 5-1 illustrates the transfer of data during an entry run. Data from the source document is keyed into the data memory. Figure 5-2 illustrates data being transferred from the data memory and written on magnetic tape *after* a record has been completely keyed in. Refer to Fig. 5-3. The data has been taken from sales orders and is to be used in a billing system. Before entering the data from Fig. 5-3, we must learn how to use two keys, the skip (SKP) and duplication (DUP) keys.

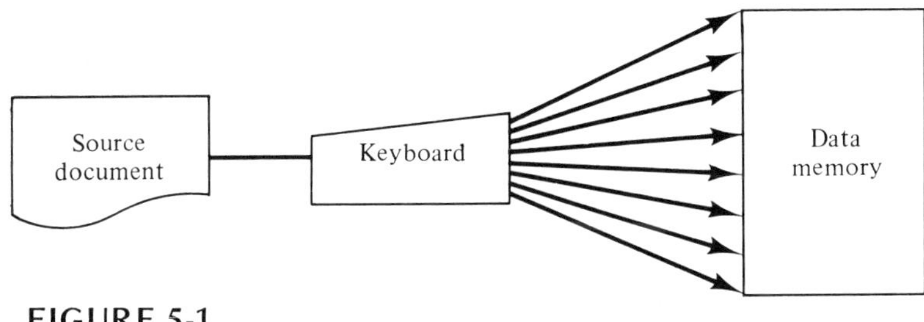

FIGURE 5-1

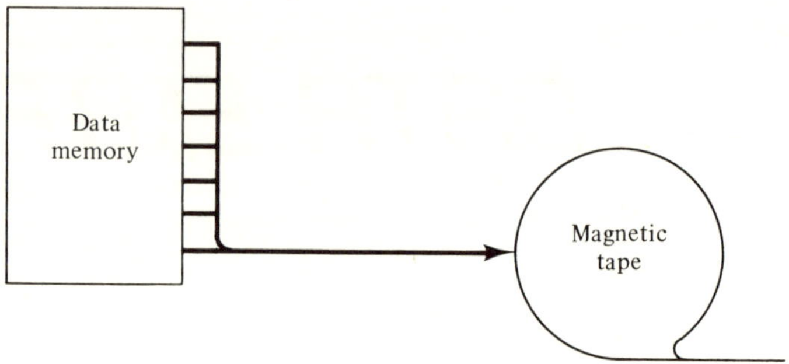

FIGURE 5-2

The SKP Key

Note that the name of customer 1, Alten Florist contains 13 characters yet the field name contains 20 positions. The remaining 7 positions must be filled with spaces by using the SKP key. After keying in ALTEN FLORIST depress the SKP key. This action enters spaces up to and including position 20. MEMORY DISPLAY will stand at position 021 and you will be ready to key in the address. (Do not key in the numbers in the column to the left of the name.)

The DUP Key

Lines 7 and 8, and lines 16 and 17 each contain two entries for the one customer. Only the sales amounts are different. To save time in entering the name, address, city, and state fields the DUP key is used. For example, assume that you have keyed record 7 into memory and it has been written on tape. You are now ready to enter record 8. Instead of rekeying GAINES TIRES 18 EAST MAIN BATAVIA, N.Y. simply depress the DUP key. Each time you depress the DUP key an entire field will be duplicated. The same procedure applies to records 16 and 17. This procedure is not valid for records 22 and 23. Pressing the DUP key for the first field of the 23rd record would result in SIMON ELECTRIC, *not* SIMON LAUNDRY because the *entire* field would be duplicated. Refer to Fig. 5-3

Source data

	Name (1 – 20)	Street (21 – 35)	City State (36 – 50)	Unused (51 – 60)	Purchases (61 – 66)		Unused (67 – 100)
1	Alten Florist	35 Miller Place	Rochester N.Y.		0423	00	
2	Browne Optician	14 Main Street	Caledonia N.Y.		0025	76	
3	Buhl Insurance	34-01 State St.	Caledonia N.Y.		0005	18	
4	Doris Dance Studio	42 Bailey St.	Buffalo N.Y.		0021	24	
5	Ebling Laundry	12 Ellicot	Batavia N.Y.		0010	55	
6	Fallsburgh Bank	4 River St.	Fallsburgh N.Y.		0100	00	
7	Gaines Tires	18 East Main	Batavia N.Y.		0084	99	
8	Gaines Tires	18 East Main	Batavia N.Y.		0025	00	
9	Jonesys Garage	11 Park Rd.	Batavia N.Y.		0006	99	
10	Kearn Mills	2343 Mill Rd.	Caledonia N.Y.		0015	50	
11	Knox Shoes	133 East Main	Batavia N.Y.		0014	75	
12	Kay Floral	77 Pearl St.	Batavia N.Y.		0010	00	
13	Kaye Drugs	6 East Town Rd.	Buffalo N.Y.		0004	00	
14	Liberty Bank	80 Main St.	Rochester N.Y.		0400	00	
15	Lowell Fence	1 School St.	Caledonia N.Y.		0235	00	
16	Martin Clothes	10 Walnut St.	Buffalo N.Y.		0035	00	
17	Martin Clothes	10 Walnut St.	Buffalo N.Y.		0022	98	
18	New York Telephone	400 Cedar St.	Batavia N.Y.		0101	55	
19	Olivers Candy	3 West Main St.	Batavia N.Y.		0008	00	
20	Panther Snowmobile	8005 Orchard	Elba N.Y.		0599	00	
21	Rays Service Center	471 Main St.	Caledonia N.Y.		0010	00	
22	Simon Electric	115 Pearl St.	Batavia N.Y.		0018	50	
23	Simon Laundry	655 Cedar St.	Buffalo N.Y.		0004	80	
24	Stanley Motors	9951 West Main	Caledonia N.Y.		0005	00	
25	Wells Real Estate	4688 State St.	Byron N.Y.		0089	00	
26	Zimmer Travel	40-33 Main St.	Buffalo N.Y.		0349	00	
27	Z B Processing	33 Bank St.	Rochester N.Y.		0018	00	

FIGURE 5-3

again. Note that under the column called PURCHASES a line has been drawn to separate the dollars and cents. *DO NOT* enter decimal points unless you have instructions to do so. Keeping track of decimal points and printing them out on reports is usually the responsibility of the computer programmer.

During the following exercises, you will hear a *double clicking* sound which occurs when the data recorder writes a record from data memory onto magnetic tape. Begin the entry run for the data in Fig. 5-3 by following the procedures given below:

DATA ENTRY PROCEDURES

Instruction	*Explanation*
1) Load Program 1	this should have been completed (See page 64)
2) POWER-ON	
3) SET SWITCH AS/DUP-OFF	to avoid skipping and duplications
4) SET SWITCH R-REL	to permit tape writing
5) SET SWITCH PL-OFF	to permit keying into data memory (This switch is OFF except when loading programs)
6) SET SWITCH M-ENT .	to begin an ENTRY operation (ENTRY means write)
7) SET SWITCH S-OFF	Since this is not a search operation the SEARCH switch *must* be OFF.
8) SET SWITCH P- as required	for this exercise set switch **P-NORMAL**
9) FEED/REWIND-LOAD	to permit threading the tape
10) Insert File Protect Ring in back of the tape reel	Remember "No ring, no write".
11) Mount the tape reel and perform the feed operation. The reflective marker on tape will be automatically positioned just before the read/write heads	

12) ER Key — put out the error lamp

13) Enter tape mark or header labels as required — not required in this exercise

14) *Key in the first data record.* Use the SKP key for skipping. When entering alphabetic characters in DUP fields depress and hold down the LTR key. Automatic release occurs when the last position is keyed. — DUP field is in numeric shift. Therefore, alphabetic characters require the LTR key.

Because the RELEASE switch is ON and the ring is inserted on the tape reel a release will occur after *all* positions in the data record have been entered into data memory.

15) Change switch M-VER.

(The first records should be verified.) — The instructor may, if he wishes, use positions 51-60 to enter the student's last name in each record keyed in this exercise. (Positions 51-60 then become a DUP field.)

16) Press ER/TBS keys — to backspace the tape one record.

17) Set switch R-REL — It should already be in this position.

18) Tap the RELease key — to read the 1st record from tape to memory.

19) Key verify all positions — key in the 1st record.

If no errors are found, automatic release will occur after the last position is keyed. Change switch M-ENT and continue the entry run. (Do not verify the remaining records in this entry run.)

Procedures if errors are found

Perform the following for each error found:

2) Depress the ER/COR keys — to permit correction of *one* character in memory.

3) Key in correct character — Enter correct character in memory

4) Verify entered record re-
   peating steps 2 and 3
   where necessary

5) Depress ER/HOM keys — Return to position 001

6) Re-verify the record — to be sure the entire record is correct. The corrected record will replace the invalid record on tape.

After the invalid record has been corrected, proceed with the keying of the rest of the file.

1) Change switch M-ENT — to enter the next record

2) Set switch R-REL — to permit records to be written on tape

3) Change switch AS/D as required — set switch AS/D-ON if you want auto skip or auto dup.

4) Depress ER/HOM keys — to begin at position 001

5) Continue with the entry run

At the end of the entry run perform the following operations:

Instruction	*Explanation*
1. Change switch AS/D-OFF	to prevent the data recorder from auto skip and auto dup.
2. Depress the ER/HOM key	to return to position 001
3. Key trailer labels	not required in this exercise
4. SET TM-W/TM	this causes a tape mark to be written at the end of your file of records. The error light will be flashing and the red EOT (end of tape) indicator will go ON.
5. SET M-VER	so that records will not be affected on rewind
6. Rewind the tape	
7. Write the number 1 on the tape container	to label your tape for future reference.

Occasionally the data recorder will not write on the tape, and this is usually due to a damaged tape or a tape that contains dust or dirt between the writing surface of the tape and the read/write head. When this occurs the status indicator signals a tape error. (See Figure 5-4)

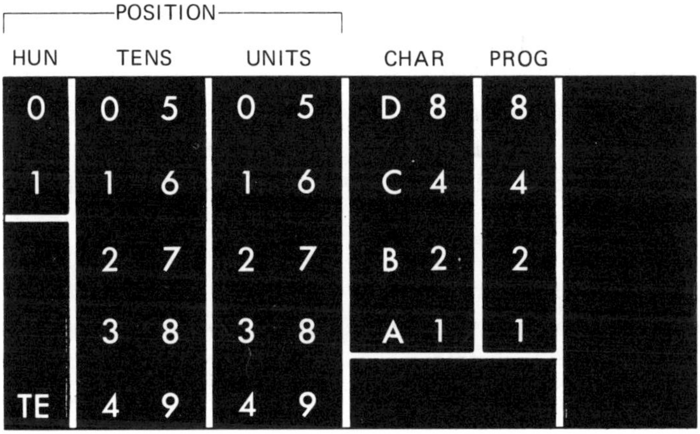

```
              POSITION
HUN    TENS    UNITS    CHAR    PROG
 0    0   5    0   5    D   8    8
 1    1   6    1   6    C   4    4
      2   7    2   7    B   2    2
      3   8    3   8    A   1    1
TE    4   9    4   9
```

FIGURE 5-4

The red letters TE (Tape Error) will go ON and the ERROR LIGHT will be flashing. If this occurs while performing the exercises in this chapter, notify your instructor or mount a new tape reel.

Left Zero-Fill

In much the same manner that the data recorder *padded* blanks out to the right to complete the unused portions of an alphabetic field it will *left fill* zeros in a numeric field if appropriate.

Assume that you must key 1234 in a six-position programmed numeric field. To insure that the entire field contained numeric characters only, you would key: ØØ1234. To give the zero-fill function to the data recorder, do the following:

1.   Key in 1234

2. Depress the LØ key, a red function key on the right hand side of the keyboard.

3. Examine MEMORY DISPLAY and note the result, ØØ1234. (use ER/MBS)

Left Zero-Fill is performed on the data recorder by first keying in the required digits, then depressing the LØ or load zero key.

It should be noted that numeric data is right-justified. That means that numeric characters are placed at the right-most side of the field. Alphabetic data, however, is left-justified or placed at the left-most side of the field. Blanks are *padded* out to the right in alphabetic fields and zeros are filled out to the left in numeric fields.

Do the following: Using the portion of the card named ALTERNATE program, prepare a Program Planning Card for Figure 5-5. Enter the program in alterate program memory. Key the data on tape using left zero-fill when needed. Each field is 5 positions long.

Position 1–5	Unused 6–20	Position 21–25	Unused 26–100
12		234	
467		54321	
90000		707	
1		45	
36		2371	
421		14389	
8052		6	
7643		00	
23		139	
17		76	
241		4231	
65		85	
721		7	
1234		44	
681		8080	

FIGURE 5-5

Chapter 6

TAPE MOVEMENT

Error recovery procedures are made easier by an understanding of the movement of the tape.

We noted earlier that when a record is completely keyed into memory an automatic release occurs. This action causes the record to be transmitted from data memory to tape and to be written on the tape. During automatic release the following takes place:

1. The tape moves forward and any previous data is erased.

2. The record in data memory is *copied* onto the erased portion of the tape as the tape moves forward under the read/write head.

3. After the record has been written, tape movement stops. See Fig. 6-1.

4. The record just written is to the left of the read/write head. The new record now exists in two places—in data memory and on the magnetic tape.

5.   The tape now moves backward to position the current record just to the right of the read/write head. See Fig. 6-2.

6.   A machine verification process now takes place. The tape moves forward and the record just written is *read* and *compared* with the record still in data memory to insure that the record on tape is the same as the record in data memory.

7.   The tape stops and the record just *read* and *compared* is to the left of the read/write head. See Figure 6-3. The tape is ready for the next record to be written.

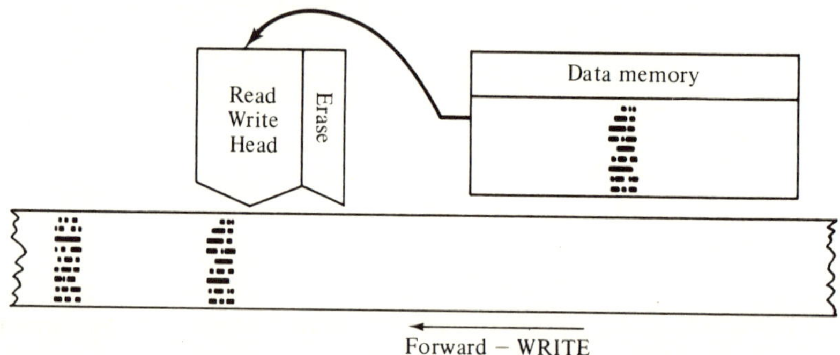

FIGURE 6-1

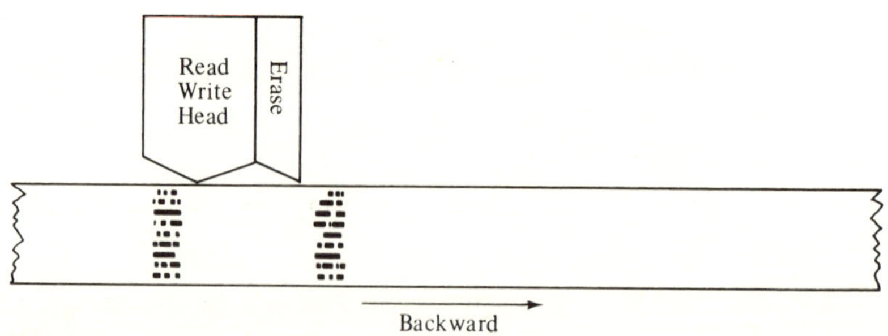

FIGURE 6-2

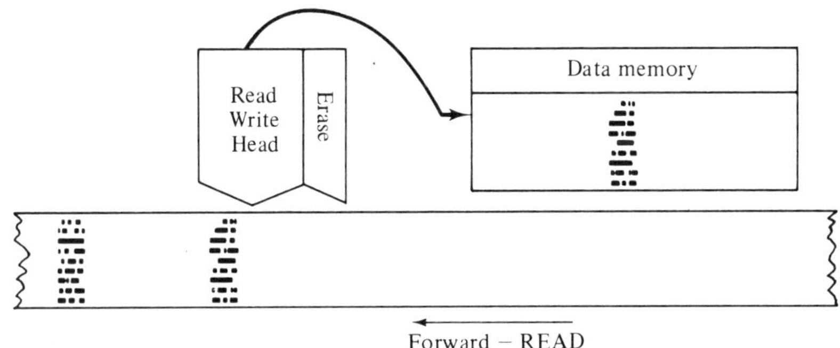

FIGURE 6-3

CORRECTING ERRORS ON TAPE

The MBS key (Memory Backspace) was used before to correct errors keyed into memory. Suppose you detect an error *after* an entire record has been written on magnetic tape? The MBS key cannot help you correct this error. You must use the tape backspace key or TBS key to correct an error written on tape. Assume that in the 13th record you have keyed JAYE DRUGS instead of KAYE DRUGS. (Because the keys J and K are next to each other this is easily possible.) Assume also that the record has just been written on tape and also exists in data memory as shown in Figure 6-4.

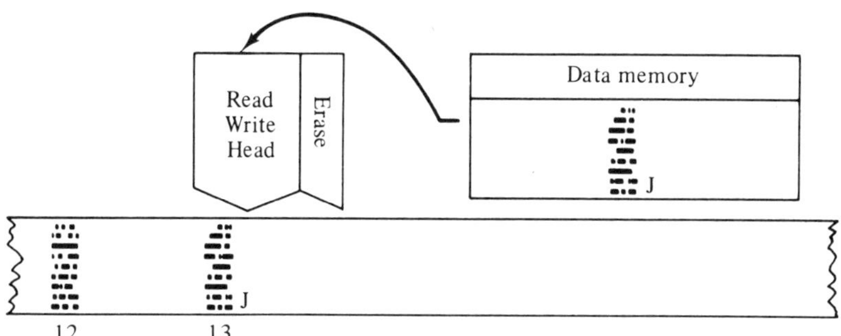

FIGURE 6-4

If you depress the ER/TBS keys the tape will back up one record length as shown in Figure 6-5.

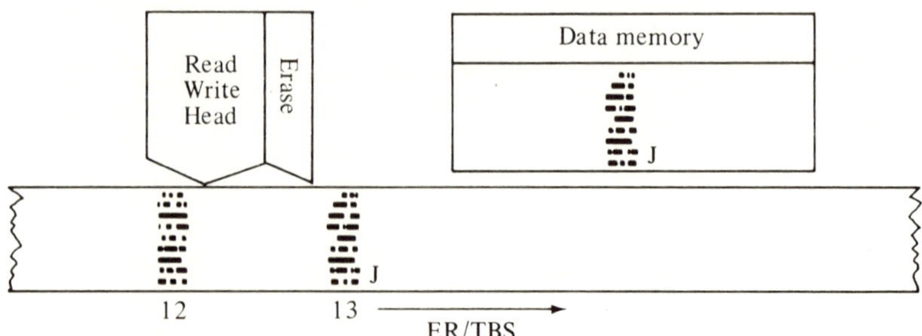

FIGURE 6-5

At this point rekey the entire record being sure to depress the K key in position 1. After the correction has been made and the entire record rekeyed, the tape will move forward erasing the invalid record. The new, correct record will be written, read and compared to the contents of data memory. You are now ready to continue the entry run.

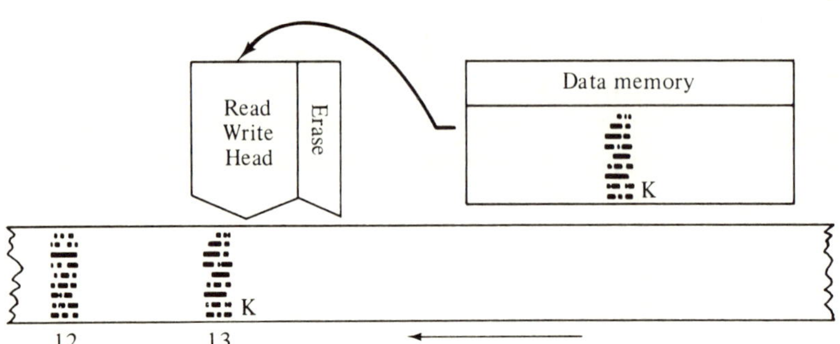

FIGURE 6-6

The data recorder may make an error when recording on magnetic tape. However, the data recorder will find its errors during the read and compare steps (Fig. 6-2 and 6-3). If a tape record and a record in data memory do not compare exactly, (and they should), the status indicator TE will come on and the ER lamp will flash.

Assume the 16th record of the document in Fig. 5-3 has just been written on to tape and the TE and ER lamps come on indicating the record written to tape is in error. (See Fig. 6-7). Because of the error condition on the tape the record must be rewritten. Perform the following:

1)　Depress the ER key to put out the ERROR lamp.

2)　Depress the RETRY switch

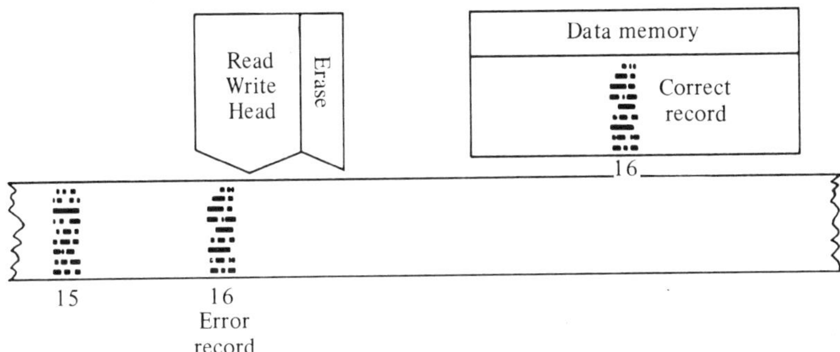

FIGURE 6-7

This causes the tape to backspace one record as shown in Figure 6-8. The error is still on the tape and the correct record is still in data memory. A *tape erase forward* takes place. The tape will move forward and the record will be erased as shown in Figure 6-9. Note that record 16 is no longer on tape, but only in the *data memory*. A *release* will occur causing record 16 to

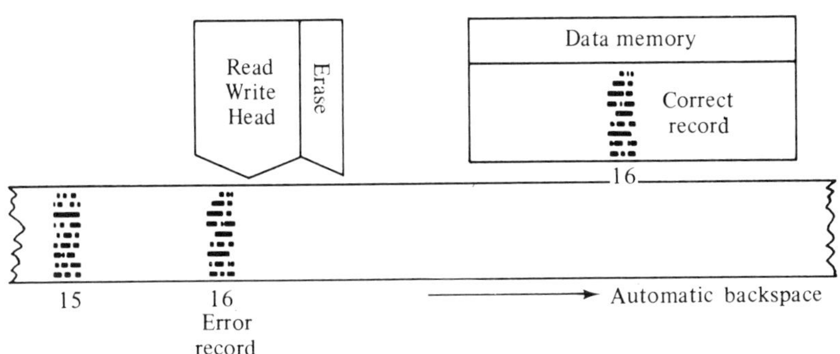

FIGURE 6-8

be written to tape as shown in Figure 6-10. The details of this procedure are also found on the STATUS INDICATOR Chart which is on the glass window of the tape deck. Look at the column headed ENTRY and opposite the error code to find the recovery procedure.

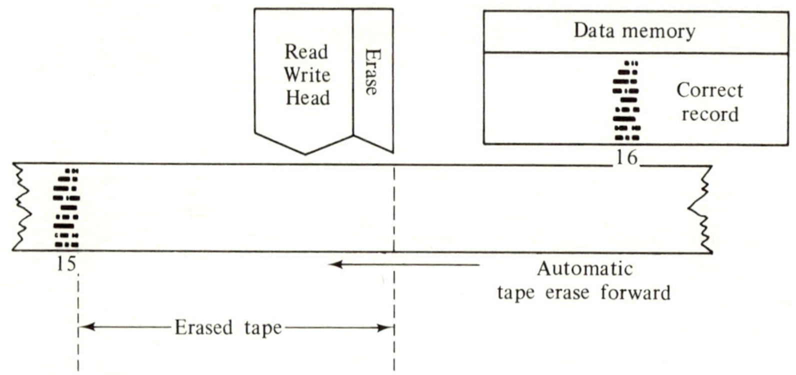

FIGURE 6-9

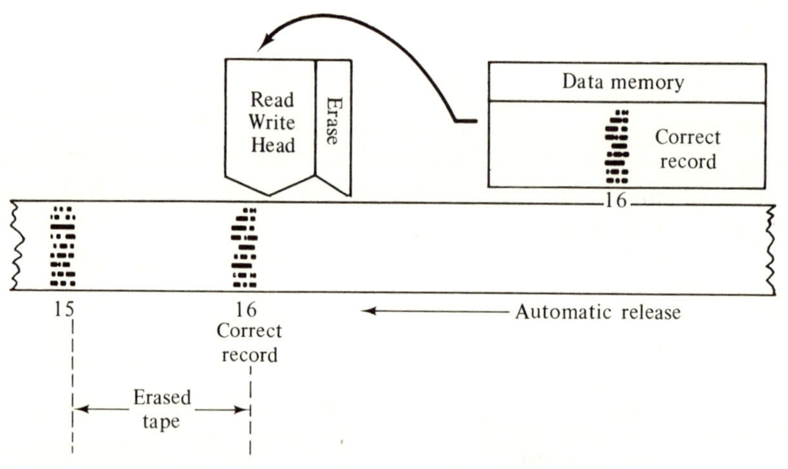

FIGURE 6-10

Chapter 7

VERIFICATION OF RECORDS

Verifying records is a process in which previously recorded tape records are checked for accuracy. Any errors made during the entry run must be corrected or eliminated.

A record to be verified is first read from magnetic tape into data memory. The operator next keys the characters in that record. Each time a character in the record is keyed, it is compared to the character located in the same position of data memory. Keying during the verification process *does not* enter new characters into *data memory*. Keying causes a comparison to be made. If a keyed character compares equally with the character in data memory, the position indicator will advance to the next position in data memory and the operator can proceed to compare the next sequential character.

After an entire record has been verified, the tape moves one record length and the next record is read into data memory. Each time a new record is read into data memory, the position indicators return to 001. The verification procedure is used to insure accuracy before the computer processes records.

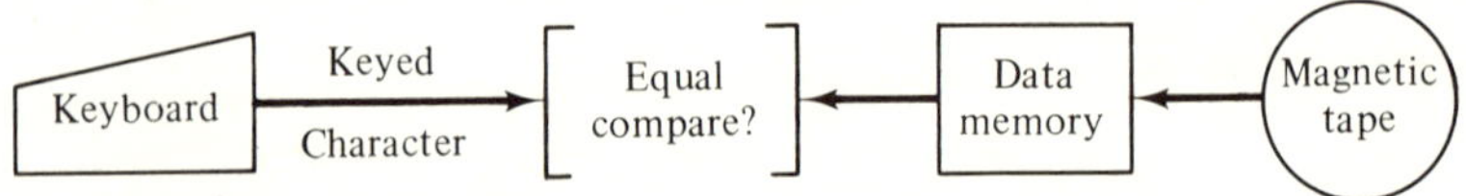

FIGURE 7-1

When an error occurs, the ERROR lamp will begin flashing and the position indicator *will not* advance.

Possible reasons for an error are:

1.   The character key just depressed is correct and the character in data memory is not.

2.   The character key just depressed is *not* correct and the character in data memory is correct.

THE LØ KEY AND VERIFICATION

If you depressed the LØ key during the *entry* run, an appropriate number of zeros were entered in the left-most portion of a numeric field. To verify that you entered numeric characters right-justified, you must perform the following:

1.   Depress the LØ key to verify the high-order (left-most) zeros.

2.   Depress the appropriate numeric keys.

Example:

Assume that ØØ123 is in a five-position field.

1.   Depress the LØ key and verify the high-order zeros (zeros are first and must be verified first).

2.   Depress the 1 key.

3.   Depress the 2 key.

4.   Depress the 3 key.

VERIFYING AUTO SKIP AND AUTO DUP FIELDS

Positions programmed for auto skip *are not* verified. They are ignored if the data recorder is under program control. However, when manually verifying auto skip fields, these positions are not ignored, they must be checked for a space character. A non-space character causes the ERROR lamp to flash during manual verification of an auto skip field.

Positions programmed for auto dup are verified by the data recorder. Characters must remain the same from record to record. If a character has changed, the *dup verify* action will stop at that character. The ER light will not be flashing. However, when manually verifying an auto dup field, the ERROR lamp will begin flashing when a character has been changed.

TAPE MOVEMENT DURING VERIFICATION

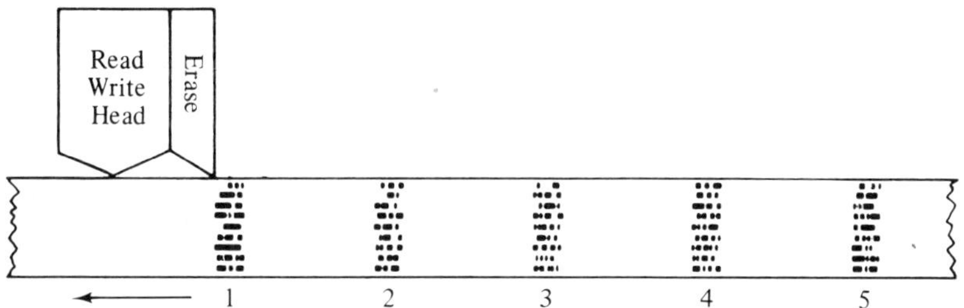

FIGURE 7-2

The position of the tape file is shown (in Figure 7-2) as it is positioned for the beginning of the verification run. During verification, the erase head is automatically turned OFF so that records cannot be erased before reading.

When verification begins, record 1 moves to the left of the read/write head as it is read into data memory as shown in Figure 7-3. When all positions are verified, record 2 is read into *data memory*. Record 1 is replaced by record 2 in data memory as shown in Figure 7-4.

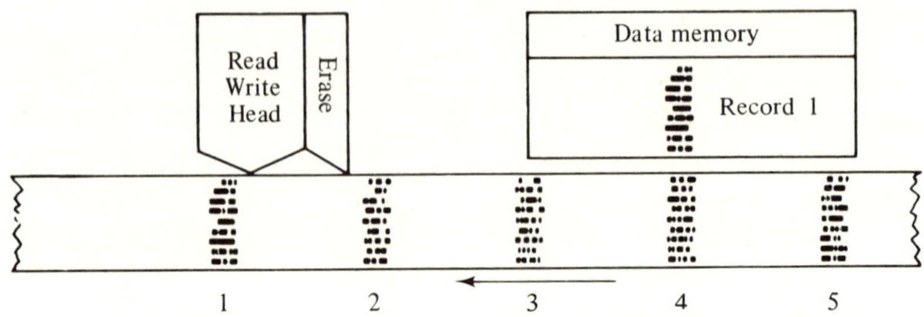

FIGURE 7-3

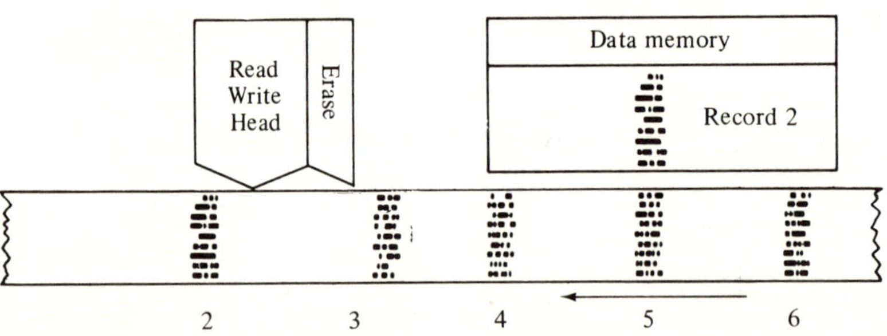

FIGURE 7-4

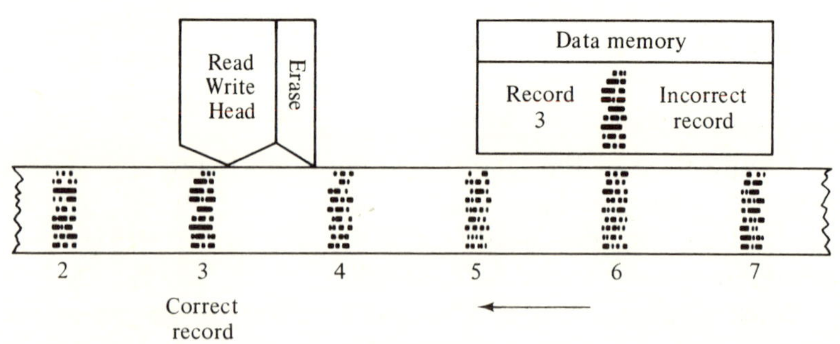

FIGURE 7-5

TAPE ERROR RECOVERY PROCEDURE DURING VERIFICATION

It is possible that the data recorder may make an error reading from tape to data memory. The machine recognizes this type of error. The error lamp will begin flashing and the TE status indicator will come on. Assume record 3 was read incorrectly and refer to Figure 7-5. Record 3 is just to the left of the read/write head. To *re-read* this record during the verification process do the following:

1. Depress the ER key to extinguish the ERROR lamp.

2. Depress the RETRY switch. This causes:

    a) The tape is backspaced one record as shown in Figure 7-6. The record causing the error is still in data memory and the correct record is on magnetic tape.

    b) The next action is an automatic *re-read* of the same record when the tape is moved forward.

3. Record 3 may now be verified.

This procedure is given on the STATUS INDICATOR Chart attached to tape deck's glass window. Look down the VERIFY/SEARCH Column opposite the error entry to locate the recovery procedure.

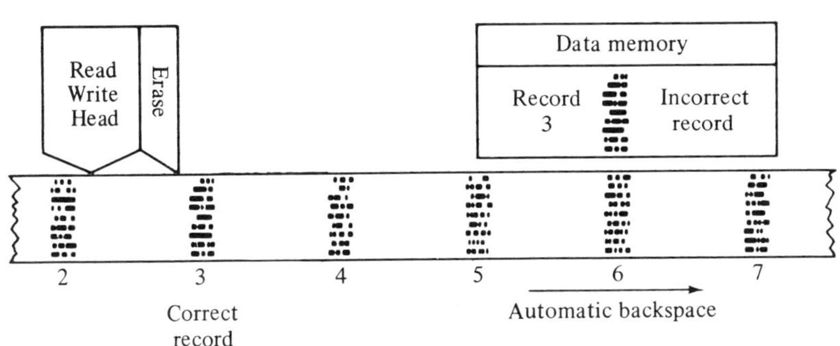

FIGURE 7-6

CORRECTING ERRORS DURING VERIFICATION

Assume that during record verification you depress a key and the ERROR lamp began flashing. You could assume that you depressed the wrong key. If after carefully depressing the appropriate key, you still do not get an equal compare, the following situation exists:

1.   The character in data memory is incorrect.

2.   The character on the tape record is also incorrect since the record was read from tape into memory.

Then you must do the following:

1.   Check the source document to be certain of the required character.

2.   Check MEMORY DISPLAY and note the character that caused the unequal compare.

Example:

If the required character is the letter A and MEMORY DISPLAY shows:

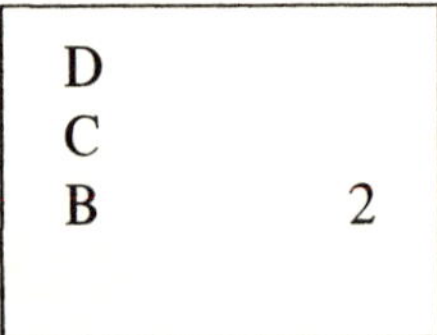

You must change the letter S in data memory and on tape to the correct letter A before continuing the verification run. (Because the keyboard is *locked out* at this time, the ER key must be depressed to turn OFF the error light and put the keyboard in a *ready* status.)

Follow these procedures to correct the error:

CORRECTION DURING VERIFICATION

Instruction	*Explanation*
1) Depress the ER/COR keys	the COR (Correction) key allows you to correct one character in data memory
2) If an entire field is in error, depress the ER/FM keys	the FM (Field Modify) key function is similar to the COR key except that an entire field may be corrected

The ER key must be depressed with the COR or FM key since COR and FM are *protected* keys.

3) Key in the correct character	the correct character is now in data memory, *not* on tape
4) Continue verification of the remainder of the record	
5) Depress ER/HOM keys (You *must* re-verify the entire record)	to re-verify the corrected record
6) Automatic release occurs when the last position is reverified	the corrected record is written out to tape *replacing* the incorrect record
7) Depress the REL key	to read the next record to be verified

When an error is found during a verification run it must:

1) Be corrected in data memory

2) Be corrected on tape.

TAPE MOVEMENT DURING A CORRECTION

Assume that record 4 has an incorrect character 3. The correct character should be 1. The release activity has read record 4 into data memory as shown in Fig. 7-7. Thus, the invalid 3 is found both on tape and in data memory. When the invalid 3 is found in data memory, the operator corrects the error by first depressing the ER/COR keys and keying in the *correct*, valid character. At this point, the 1 is in data memory but the invalid 3 is still on tape as shown in Fig. 7-8. Verification of the rest of the record continues. When verification is completed *no* release takes place. Because the ER/COR keys were depressed, auto release is prevented.

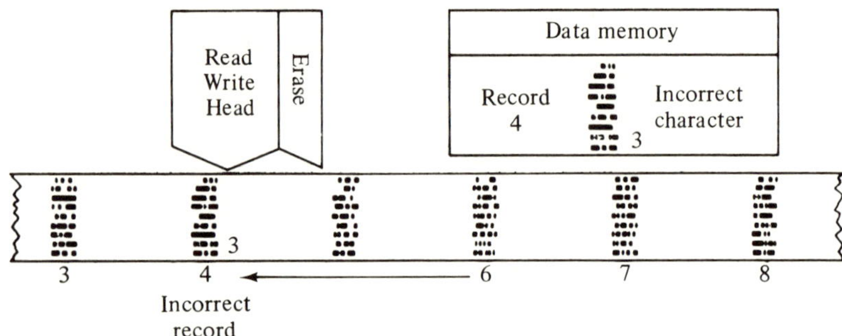

FIGURE 7-7

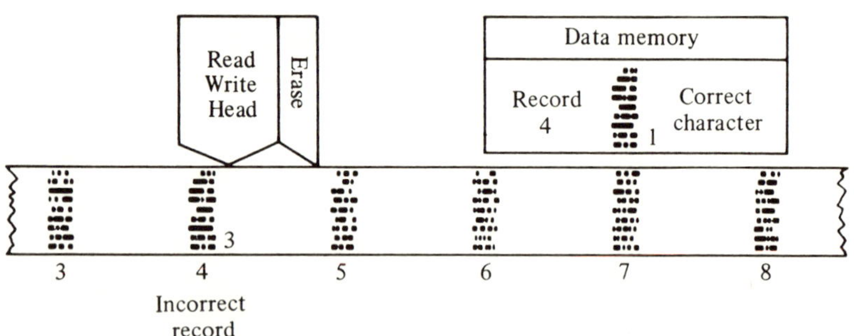

FIGURE 7-8

To erase the incorrect tape record, you must:

1) Depress the ER/HOM keys

2) Re-verify the entire record. When the entire record has been reverified *and no errors are found*, an automatic

backspace occurs on tape. (See figure 7-9). Next an automatic release occurs erasing the invalid tape record and writing the valid record in its place. (See Fig. 7-10). A read-after-write check moves the tape backward (as during an entry run) as shown in Fig. 7-11. The tape is next read and machine verified as the tape moves forward. To access the next record (5) in the file for verification, the REL key must be depressed. (See Fig. 7-13).

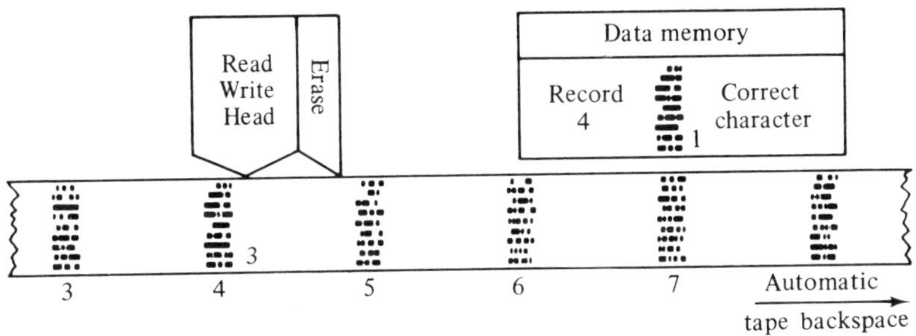

FIGURE 7-9

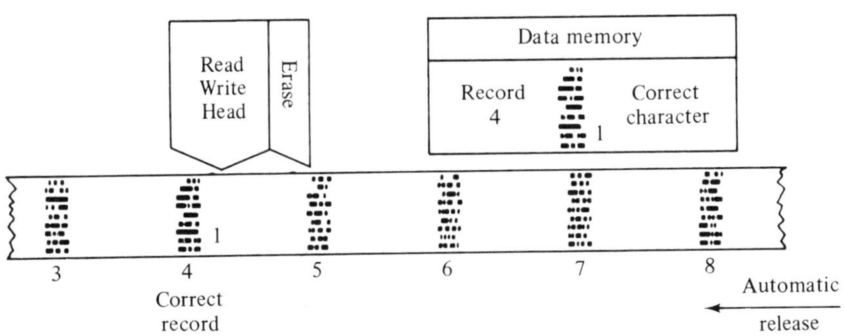

FIGURE 7-10

TAPE ERRORS

You have already prepared a tape file of records in Chapter 5 and named the tape as Tape-1. You prepared the program planning card for this file in Chapter 4 page 61. Change this

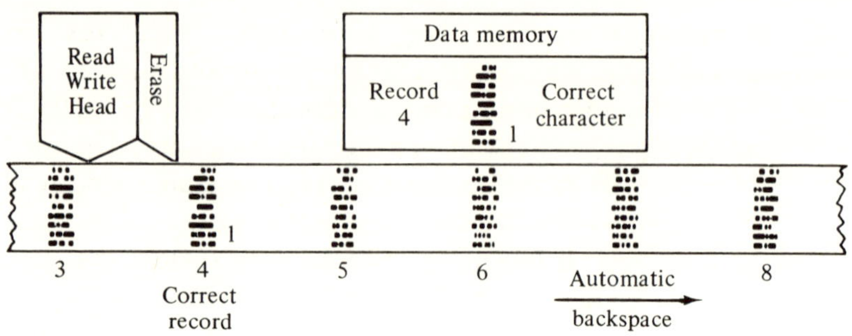

FIGURE 7-11

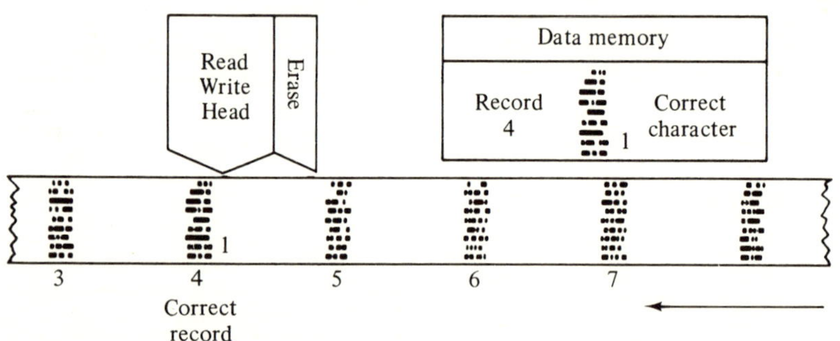

FIGURE 7-12

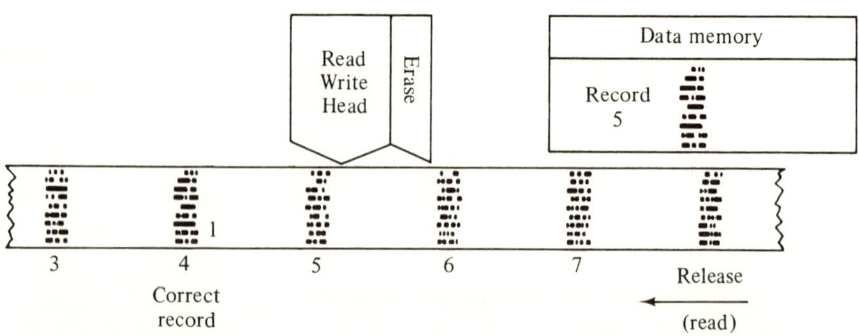

FIGURE 7-13

program planning card to specify an AUTO DUP field in positions 1-20. Refer to Figure 5-3 and compare it to Figure 7-14. Errors have been deliberately made in some of the records in Figure 5-3 for you to catch now and correct. Note that records 7, and 8, 16 and 17 must be verified in the auto dup fields (positions 1 to 20). Before proceeding to the verify run, review these instructions and their explanations.

CORRECTING A SINGLE CHARACTER

Instruction	*Explanation*
1) Determine the correct character and its position	
2) ER/COR keys	to allow entry of the correct character
3) Enter the correct data item	
4) Continue verification	use steps 2 and 3 above for any invalid character
5) ER/HOM keys	begin at position 001
6) Reverify the entire record. (If errors reoccur repeat steps 1-6 above)	auto release occurs if reverified record is correct
7) REL key	to read next record to be verified into data memory
8) Continue with verification run	

CORRECTING AN ENTIRE FIELD

Instruction	*Explanation*
1) Determine the field and the correct data item for that field and change SWITCH AS/D OFF	prevent auto skip auto dup
2) ER/FM keys	to change characters in data memory
3) Enter the correct data item	
4) Continue verification	

After the entire record is verified and corrected

5) ER/HOM keys — begin at position 001

6) Reverify the entire record. (If errors reoccur repeat steps 1-6 above) — auto release occurs when entire record is correct and reverified.

7) REL key — to read next record to be verified into data memory

8) Change switch AS/D — as required

9) Continue with verification run

Source Data

Name (1 – 20)	Street (21 – 35)	City State (35 – 50)	Unused (56 – 60)	Purchases (61 – 66)	Unused (67 – 100)
1 Alter Florist	35 Miller Place	**Rochester, N.Y.**		42300	
2 Browne Optician	14 Main Street	Caledonia N.Y.		2576	
3 Buhl Insurance	34-01 State St.	Caledonia N.Y.		518	
4 Doris Dance Studio	42 Bailey St.	Buffalo N.Y.		2144	
5 Ebling Laundry	12 Ellicot	Batavia N.Y.		1055	
6 Fallsburgh Bank	4 River St.	Fallsburgh N.Y.		10000	
7 Gaines Tires	18 East Main St.	Batavia N.Y.		8499	
8 Gaines Tires	18 East Main St.	Batavia N.Y.		2500	
9 Jonesys Garage	11 Park Rd.	Batavia N.Y.		699	
10 Kearn Mills	2343 Mill Rd.	Caledonia N.Y.		1500	
11 Knox Shoes	133 East Main	Batavia N.Y.		1475	
12 Kay Floral	77 Pearl St.	Batavia N.Y.		1000	
13 Kaye Drugs	6 East Town Rd.	Buffalo N.Y.		400	
14 Liberty Bank	80 Main St.	Rochester N.Y.		40000	
15 Lowell Fence	10 School St.	Caledonia N.Y.		23500	
16 Martin Clothes	10 Walnut St.	Buffalo N.Y.		3500	
17 Martin Clothes	10 Walnut St.	Buffalo N.Y.		2298	
18 New York Telephone	400 Cedar St.	Batavia N.Y.		10155	
19 Olivers Candy	3 West Main St.	Batavia N.Y.		800	
20 Panther Snowmobile	8005 Orchard	Elba N.Y.		59900	
21 Rays Service Center	471 Main St.	Caledonia N.Y.		1000	
22 Simon Electric	115 Pearl St.	Batavia N.Y.		1850	
23 Simon Laundry	655 Cedar St.	Buffalo N.Y.		480	
24 Stanley Motors	9951 West Main	Batavia N.Y.		500	
25 Wells Real Estate	4688 State St.	Byron N.Y.		8900	
26 Zimmer Travel	40-33 Main St.	Buffalo N.Y.		34900	
27 Z B Processing	31 Bank St.	Rochester N.Y.		1800	

FIGURE 7-14

*Note: the REL key is depressed for the first record in a file and for the next sequential record which follows a *corrected* record.

You should now be ready to verify Figure 7-14. Remember Figure 7-14 is not exactly like Figure 5-3. Some of the data items in Figure 5-3 have been varied, creating errors on tape. These errors *must* be corrected using Figure 7-14. When you complete the verification run, the tape file must be exactly like Figure 7-14.

VERIFICATION RUN

Instruction	*Explanation*
1) Load Program	
2) POWER-ON	
3) SET SWITCHES	
AS/D — OFF	to prevent auto skip and auto dup.
	to allow release
R — REL	(not loading a program)
PL — OFF	to verify
M — VER	(not performing a search)
S — OFF	NORMAL recommended
P — as required	to thread tape to be verified
FEED/REWIND-LOAD	Tape records cannot be accidently erased (no ring, no write)
4) Remove the file–protect ring from the back of the tape reel	
5) Mount the tape reel. Perform a tape feed operation	the reflective marker will be automatically positioned
6) ER key	to extinguish the ERROR lamp
7) REL key	to read first record from tape to data memory.
If the EOT indicator is on and the ERROR lamp is flashing	There is a tape mark at the beginning of the tape.
Depress the ER key	to extinguish the ERROR lamp
Move TM switch to C/TM	to clear the tape mark from data memory
Depress the REL key	to read the next record into data memory

8) Key-verify header labels (There are no header labels in exercise 1. continue with step 9.)

header labels are verified before verification of records.

9) Verify the records
Use SKP for skipped fields
Hold down the LTR key when verifying alphabetical characters in a DUP field.

the NAME field in records 7 and 16 must be verified since they are the first of two duplicate names. The auto dup field will change on all records except records 8 and 17. Therefore *manually* verify positions 1 to 20 for all records except records 8 and 17.

for records 8 and 17 use the DUP key or SET AS/DUP-ON. If your instructor had you place your name in positions 51-60, this field must also be verified as a DUP field.

10) Change switch AS/D

as required for auto skip or auto dup fields.

11) ER/HOM keys

to begin from the *first position to be verified*, note that if you skip the first field the beginning position will be 021 not 001.

AT THE END OF THE VERIFICATION RUN

12) AS/D-OFF

to prevent auto skip and auto dup

13) Verify trailer labels
There are no trailer labels for exercise 1. However, you did place a tape mark at the end of the file of records for exercise 1. Therefore, the EOT indicator should be lit and the ERROR lamp should be flashing. Turn the ERROR lamp off.

Exercises

1. Prepare an appropriate program card and enter data items on tape and enter a tape mark after the last record for the following file of sales invoices (Figure 7-15). Verify the file on tape. Note that each record in this file is identified by an X keyed into position 80. Further, no decimal point is to be entered to separate dollars from cents. Lable the tape as TAPE 2.

							80
Product	Date	Invoice number	Customer number	Quantity	Unit price		X
Table	121172	48763	00138	015	0024	00	
Chairs	121172	48764	00138	060	0015	00	
Desk	121272	38575	12202	004	0300	00	
Bookcase	011973	33575	11322	002	0029	00	
Desk light	011873	38588	20037	004	0018	00	
Coat rack	011873	38600	20038	002	0012	00	
Chalkboard	011873	38601	20039	001	0179	00	
Bulletin board	011873	38608	20040	002	0020	00	
Book rack	011873	38629	20041	060	0018	00	
Gliders	011373	35500	21455	120	0005	00	

Figure 7-15

Plant and equipment record

Job peq

Room location	Item number	Description	Acquistion date	Retirement date	Total cost		Periodic depreciation	
B340	01634	Drill press	02/65	02/75	1200	00	120	00
C551	02226	Grinder	03/65	02/75	1500	00	150	00
C551	03884	Sander	03/65	02/75	0040	00	004	00
C551	03886	Sand paper	09/65	06/75	0015	00	001	50
B220	11430	Truck	12/70	12/78	5000	00	500	00
B220	67889	Trailer	12/70	12/78	0700	00	070	00
B220	84228	Lathes	12/70	12/80	3500	00	350	00
B193	22439	Welding torch	01/71	01/76	0100	00	010	00
B193	00788	Furnace	01/71	01/85	0500	00	050	00
C660	11577	Jigsaw	04/71	04/77	0100	00	010	00

Figure 7-16

2. Prepare an appropriate program card and enter data items on tape for the file of plant and equipment records shown in Figure 7-16 and verify the tape file. The job file name PEQ must be entered into the first three positions of each record. Design your own program to enter these data items. Remember, the length of any single field must be long enough to contain the largest data item to be entered in that field. The record length is 80 characters.

PROGRAM CODES 6 AND 7, PROGRAMMED LEFT-ZERO FUNCTION

Program codes 6 and 7 perform exactly the same left-zero functions. Recall that in program planning a five-position numeric field was coded as 2ƀƀƀƀ. To enter a numeric data item into this field you keyed the numbers and depressed the LØ key. If you forgot to depress the LØ key, errors could exist on tape. Using the *programmed left zero function*, another field cannot be keyed in unless the LØ key was depressed. If the LØ key is not depressed, the ERROR light will flash.

Enter a program into the MAIN memory with either a 6 or 7 in the first position of the numeric field. For example, key in: 6ƀƀƀƀ or 7ƀƀƀƀ in two adjacent numeric fields.

Assume that 123 is to be keyed into the five position programmed left-zero numeric field, followed by 1234 to be keyed into the next adjacent 5 position left-zero numeric field.

> First key 123
> Omit the LØ key
> Attempt to key in 1234
> When you hit the 1st position of the second field,
> the ERROR light will begin flashing

To correct this error use the ER/MBS keys, key in 123, depress the LØ key, and continue on in the job.

Exercise

Create a program planning card for the following material:
(Amount is to be programmed as a left-zero numeric field)

Field Name	*Positions*	*Data Type*
Amount	1 - 6	Numeric
Skip	7 - 80	Auto Skip

Load the program into the MAIN memory
Perform a entry and verification run on the following data items:

140

21

1259

76040

3

Note the automatic verification for the field named Amount.

Chapter 8

PROGRAM TAPE STRIPS

Programs can be stored permanently on strips of magnetic tape. Once a program is created and stored on a strip of magnetic tape, it may be used whenever needed by simply reading it into the program memory of any data recorder. Sharing these programs saves the time required by operators to create duplicate programs and an activity such as preparing billing information can be performed by several operators simultaneously if the programs are duplicated and kept in program libraries.

Program tape strips are used most efficiently when they are stored on a reel of library programs and entered into program memory before mounting a file reel for an entry run.

MAKING THE TAPE STRIPS

To make the program tape strip use a four foot length of magnetic tape (Fig. 8-1). Make a 3/4" fold as shown in Fig. 8-1 .

The *shiny* non-oxide side of the tape must be on the inside. Seal the fold with a gummed label as shown in Fig. 8-2. Place a reflective marker about two feet from the unfolded end of the tape on the shiny side.

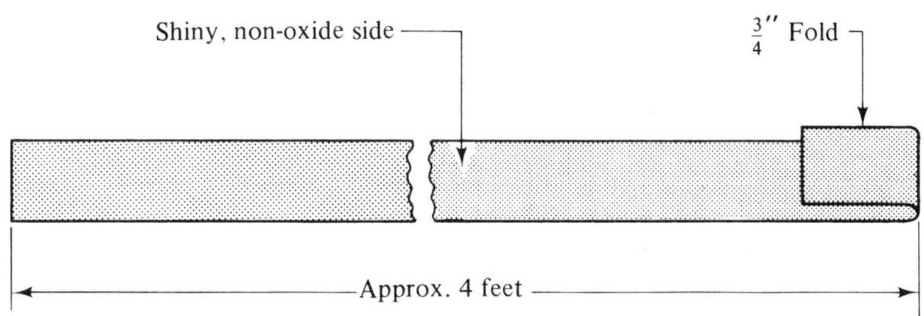

FIGURE 8-1

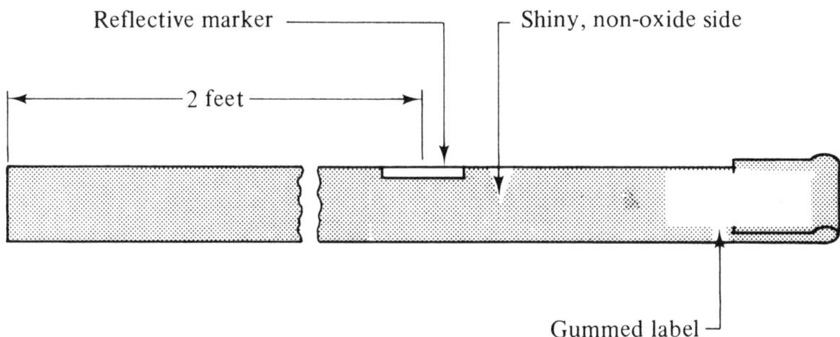

FIGURE 8-2

WRITING A PROGRAM ON THE TAPE STRIP

After creating the tape strip it is ready to accept a program. Earlier you wrote a program for the billing information found in Fig. 5-3. Using the program planning card of exercise 2, page 61 , write a program tape using the following instructions:

PROCEDURES FOR WRITING
ONE PROGRAM ON A TAPE STRIP

Instructions	*Explanations*
1) POWER-ON	
2) SET SWITCH AS/D-OFF	to avoid auto skip and auto dup
3) SET SWITCH R-REL	for automatic release of the program from memory to tape
4) SET SWITCH PL-OFF	while keying the program
5) SET SWITCH M-ENT	this program will be written in *data memory*
6) SET SWITCH S-OFF	no search is to be performed at this time
7) SET SWITCH P-NORMAL	recommended for this operation
8) FEED/REWIND–LOAD	to thread tape
9) Insert the file protect ring and mount the tape	this extinguishes the FPR (File Protect Lamp)
10) Thread the program tape	
11) Mount the program tape with the reflector marker face down	the tape must stop when the reflective marker is positioned before the Read/Write head (Fig. 8-3)
12) Depress the ER key	to extinguish the ER lamp
13) Hold the NUM key down and enter the program of exercise 2, page 62. ıto release occurs when the last position is keyed and the program will be written on tape. A key must be depressed for each memory position. (Use the space bar where appropriate)	the NUM key overrides any positions programmed for alphabetic positions *NOTE:* the program is *not* loaded into *program memory*. You are performing a data transfer activity from *data memory* to tape.
14) SET SWITCH TM-W/TM	write a tape mark at the end of the program.
15) Change SWITCH M-VER	to verify the program

16) Reposition the program tape strip. The reflective marker you placed on the tape should stop before the read/write head.

to begin verification

17) Perform a tape feed operation

18) Depress the ER key

to extinguish the ER lamp

19) Depress the REL key

to load the program from tape into data memory for verification

20) Hold the NUM key down during verification. When the last position is keyed, auto release will occur. The tape mark record will also be read into data memory causing the ER lamp to flash and the EOT indicator to go ON.

to verify the program by comparing data memory to key depression (Data memory now holds the program loaded from tape.)

Error Correction
for each error found

21) Depress the ER/COR keys

the change characters in data memory

22) Hold the NUM key down as the correct character is depressed

to override any position programmed for alphabetic characters

After the entire program has been verified and corrected

23) Depress ER/HOM keys

to begin at position 001

24) Re-verify the entire program

to insure that corrections are right The corrected program will be written on tape

25) Change SWITCH FEED/REWIND-LOAD

before removing the program tape

26) Remove the program tape

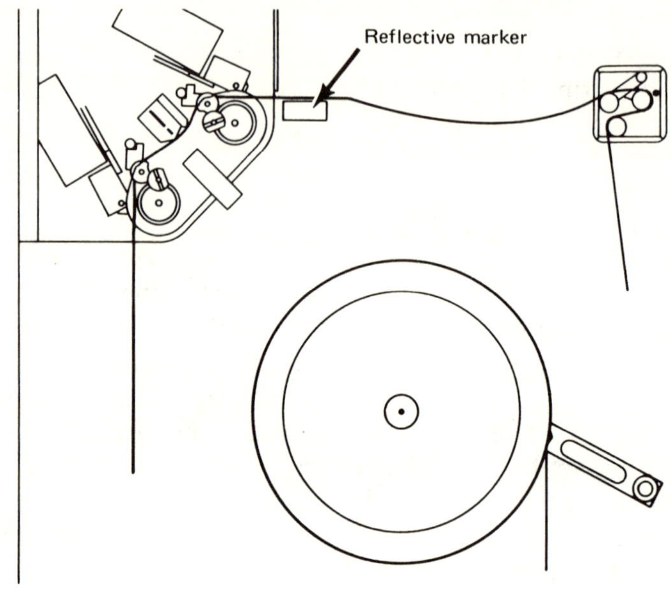

FIGURE 8-3

LOADING A PROGRAM FROM A PROGRAM TAPE STRIP

Using the program tape strip of exercise 2, load your program into program memory. Do the following:

Instructions   *Explanations*

1) **POWER-ON**
   (extinguish the ER lamps)
2) **SET SWITCHES:**

AS/D – OFF	to avoid auto skip and auto dup
R – REL	to permit automatic release
PL – PROG LOAD	to load the program
M – VER	to read from tape (VERIFY READ)
S – OFF	no search to be performed now
P – NORMAL	recommended
FEED/REWIND–LOAD	to thread the program tape

3) Load the tape, reflector to properly position the tape
   mark down
4) Perform a tape feed operation, (extinguish the ER
   lamp)

TO LOAD *ONE* PROGRAM

5) Depress the PRG key to MAIN is recommended for
   MAIN or ALTERNATE   this exercise
6) Depress the REL key   to read the program from tape
                             to *program memory*
7) Change SWITCH PL-OFF   after the program has been
                             loaded turn the PROGRAM
                             LOAD switch OFF
8) Change SWITCH FEED/   to remove the program tape
   REWIND-LOAD
9) Remove the program tape

TO VERIFY THAT THE PROGRAM IS PROPERLY LOADED DO THE FOLLOWING:

1) SET SWITCHES:
   AS/D – OFF
      R – OFF
     PL – OFF
      M – VER
      S – OFF
      P – NORMAL
2) Depress the ER/HOM keys
3) Verify the program memory
   display and compare each
   character in program memory to the program planning card for exercise two

Exercise

1) Create a program tape for exercise 3, page 62.

2) The following program card (Figure 8-4) contains a MAIN program and an ALTERNATE program. Create two programs on tape, load into MAIN and ALTERNATE program memory and verify.

Hint: Create two records on tape, write the tape mark.

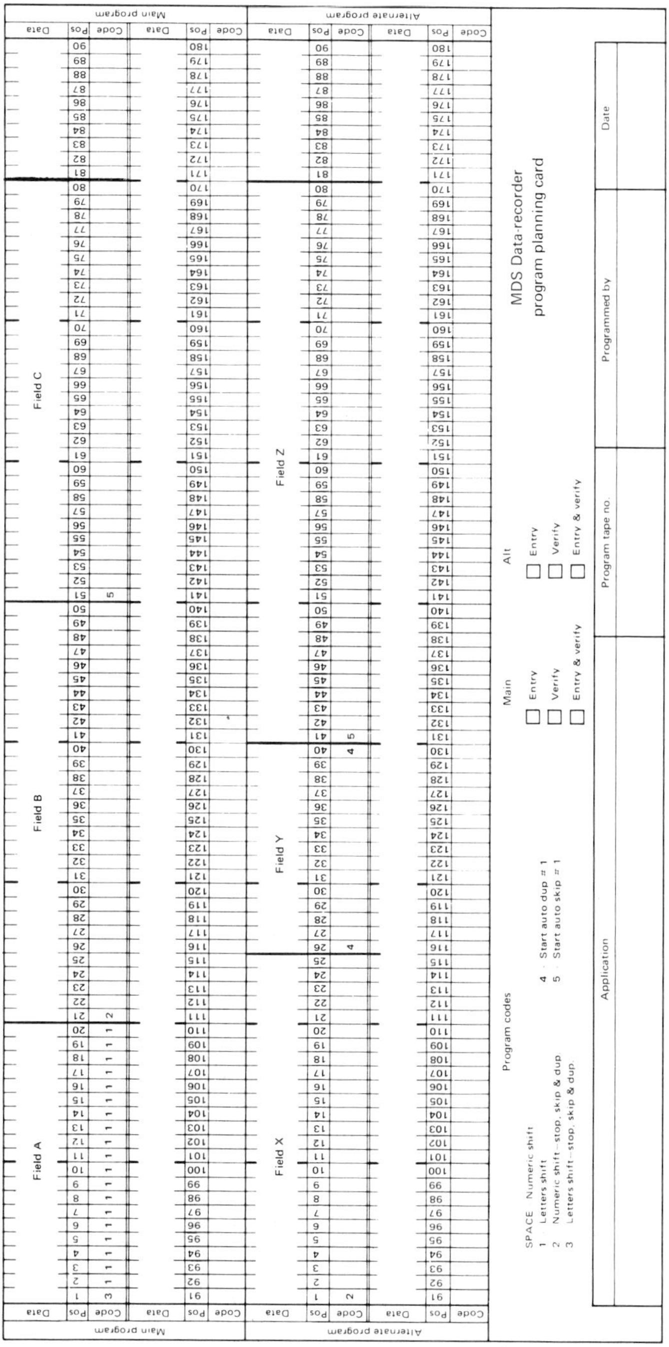

MDS Data-recorder
program planning card

Programmed by

Date

Program tape no.

Main
- ☐ Entry
- ☐ Verify
- ☐ Entry & verify

Alt
- ☐ Entry
- ☐ Verify
- ☐ Entry & verify

Application

Program codes

SPACE Numeric shift
1 Letters shift
2 Numeric shift—stop, skip & dup
3 Letters shift—stop, skip & dup.
4 · Start auto dup ≠ 1
5 · Start auto skip ≠ 1

Main program — Field A, Field B, Field C (Code, Pos, Data)
Alternate program — Field X, Field Y, Field Z (Code, Pos, Data)

Figure 8-4

Chapter **9**

SEARCH

The data recorder can search for a specific record on tape. However, two items are required before a search can be made:

1) The tape reel containing the desired record

2) The record identification

A record identification is simply a field containing a data item unique to a record—an employee number, a social security number, etc.

The identification (ID) is used to locate:

1) a record in a file of records

2) the last record in a file in order to add new records or to verify new records that have been added.

The record ID must be in the same field (positions) for every record in the file. For example, if the record ID (sometimes called the identifier) is a social security number nine characters long, the same 9 positions in each record in that file must be used for the social security number. If the social security number appears in positions 21-29 in the first record, it must appear in positions 21-29 in all succeeding records in that file.

Assume an 80-position record to be searched on a social security number. To begin a search operation, the social security number for the desired record must be *keyed into data memory positions 21-29.* Spaces must be keyed in positions 1-20 and positions 30-80.

When the search operation is executed, each record is examined *sequentially* from the beginning of the file and the field containing social security numbers will be *compared* to the record ID in data memory. When an equal compare is found, the search operation will be completed. Fig. 9-1 shows that record 8 contains the record ID desired. Fig. 9-1 also shows the position of record 8 on the tape in relation to the read/write head *after* the search operation is completed. The desired record *has not* been read into data memory. The data memory contains the identifier *only*.

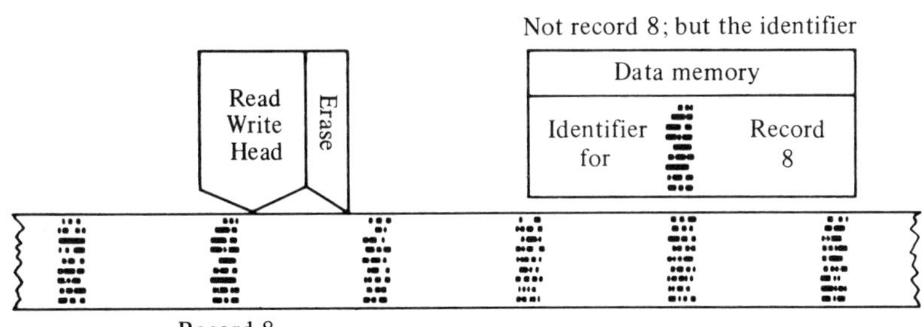

FIGURE 9-1

Exercise

Perform a *search* for record 5 of Exercise 1 Chap. 7 on Tape 2 using customer number 20037 as the record ID and the following instructions:

Instructions	*Explanation*

1) POWER-ON
2) SET SWITCHES
    AS/D — OFF — to prevent auto skip and auto dup

    R — OFF — to prevent a release
    PL — OFF — (not loading a program)
    M — VER — to prevent accidentally erasing tape

    S — OFF — the search has yet not been started

    P — NORMAL — recommended
FEED/REWIND-LOAD — to thread the tape

3) *IF* an entry run is to follow the search:

    Insert the file protect ring — to write on tape

    IF a verification run is to follow the search:

    Remove the file protect ring — to avoid erasing tape

4) Mount the tape reel — the reflective marker is automatically positioned
Perform a tape feed operation

5) ER key — to extinguish the error lamp
6) Change SWITCH M-ENT — to key in record ID

7) Key in the record ID — needed for search operation
Key *spaces* in all other positions in the record

8) Change SWITCH M-VER — to verify the identifier
9) ER/HOM keys — to begin from position 001
10) Verify the identifier

IF YOU HAVE MADE AN ERROR IN THE IDENTIFIER DO THE FOLLOWING:

change SWITCH M-ENT	to key into data memory
key the correct character	
change SWITCH M-VER	to continue verifying the identifier.

11) Change SWITCHES

S – SEARCH	to begin the search
R – REL	to permit release
M – VER	to allow the data recorder to read and verify.

12) Hold the REL key down for about one second — the tape search operation will begin when this key is released.

When the record is found the search operation is complete. *No* error indicators will be ON. If a tape error is encountered, the ERROR light will be flashing and the TE indicator will be ON. In this situation, do the following:

Depress the RETRY switch   the tape search will start again

After you located record 5, verify the data record found.

13) Change SWITCHES

AS/ D-OFF	(if you want to auto skip or auto dup SET SWITCH AS/D-ON)
S-OFF	the search has been completed

14) Depress the RETRY switch — the tape will backspace one record length to read the desired record into data memory (See Fig. 9-1)

15) Change SWITCH R-OFF   to avoid release

16) Verify the data   to insure you have the desired record

To search for a tape mark, follow the same steps given above , *omitting* steps 13, 14, 15 and 16.

Exercise:

Search for the tape mark you created on tape-2.

17)	ER key	to extinguish the **ERROR** light
18)	Verify the tape mark by DEPRESSING the RETRY switch.	the code for a tape mark is A21

Exercises:

1) Perform a search operation for record 15 in Figure 7-14.

2) The search may be used to change or update any data item. Perform a search operation on record 16 in Figure 7-14 and update the purchase amounts to 0.00.

3) Using Figure 9-2 update purchases for the file created in Figure 5-3 and verified in Figure 7-14.

Name (1 – 20)	Street (31 – 35)	City State (36 – 50)	Unused (51 – 60)	Purchases (61 – 66)	Unused (67 – 100)
1 Alter Florist	35 Miller Place	**Rochester, N.Y.**		40300	
2 Browne Optician	14 Main Street	Caledonia N.Y.		3509	
3 Buhl Insurance	34-01 State St.	Caledonia N.Y.		618	
4 Doris Dance Studio	42 Bailey St.	Buffalo N.Y.		1145	
5 Ebling Laundry	12 Ellicot	Batavia N.Y.		1222	
6 Fallsburgh Bank	4 River St.	Fallsburgh N.Y.		98888	
7 Gaines Tires	18 East Main St.	Batavia N.Y.		8700	
8 Gaines Tires	18 East Main St.	Batavia N.Y.		3500	
9 Jonesys Garage	11 Park Rd.	Batavia N.Y.		700	
10 Kearn Mills	2343 Mill Rd.	Caledonia N.Y.		2050	
11 Knox Shoes	133 East Main	Batavia N.Y.		1400	
12 Kay Floral	77 Pearl St.	Batavia N.Y.		2000	
13 Kaye Drugs	6 East Town Rd.	Buffalo N.Y.		300	
14 Liberty Bank	80 Main St.	Rochester N.Y.		32000	
15 Lowell Fence	**10 School St.**	Caledonia N.Y.		13515	
16 Martin Clothes	10 Walnut St.	Buffalo N.Y.		3895	
17 Martin Clothes	10 Walnut St.	Buffalo N.Y.		3450	
18 New York Telephone	400 Cedar St.	Batavia N.Y.		2879	
19 Olivers Candy	3 West Main St.	Batavia N.Y.		600	
20 Panther Snowmobile	8005 Orchard	Elba N.Y.		60000	
21 Rays Service Center	**471 Main St.**	Caledonia N.Y.		2300	
22 Simon Electric	115 Pearl St.	Batavia N.Y.		1500	
23 Simon Laundry	655 Cedar St.	Buffalo N.Y.		380	
24 Stanley Motors	9951 West Main	**Batavia, N.Y.**		499	
25 Wells Real Estate	4688 State St.	Byron N.Y.		7900	
26 Zimmer Travel	40-33 Main St.	Buffalo N.Y.		43900	
27 Z B Processing	31 Bank St.	Rochester N.Y.		1700	

FIGURE 9-2

Chapter 10

ALTERNATE PROGRAMS

Consider two 80-column formats for a payroll. Personal information is entered in format 1, payroll information in format 2.

FORMAT 1

Field Name	Positions	Data Type
Social Security Number	1 - 9	Numeric
Employee Name	10 - 25	Alphabetic
Employee Address	26 - 40	Alphabetic
City and State	41 - 60	Alphabetic
Zip Code	61 - 65	Numeric
Marital Status	66 - 66	Alphabetic
Dependents	67 - 68	Numeric
Employee Type	69 - 70	Numeric
Employee Number	71 - 75	Numeric
Security Classification	76 - 76	Alphabetic
Skip	77 - 79	Auto Skip
Format ID	80 - 80	Numeric

FORMAT 2

Field Name	*Positions*	*Data Type*
Rate	1 - 4	Numeric
Hours	5 - 8	Numeric
Overtime	9 - 12	Numeric
Year to Date gross	13 - 19	Numeric
Year to Date FICA*	20 - 24	Auto Skip
Year to Date State Tax*	25 - 30	Auto Skip
Year to Date Federal Tax*	31 - 36	Auto Skip
Vacation Pay	37 - 42	Numeric
Health Insurance	43 - 47	Numeric
Union Dues	48 - 51	Numeric
Retirement	52 - 56	Numeric
Skip	57 - 70	Auto Skip
Employee Number	71 - 75	Numeric
Building	76 - 79	Alphabetic
Format ID	80 - 80	Numeric

These two formats constitute one payroll record for each employee.

*To be filled with blanks. Taxes will be calculated by a computer program.

Exercise 1

Prepare a program planning card using Format 1 as the MAIN program and Format 2 as the ALTERNATE program. Enter both programs into program memory.

PROGRAM CONTROL FOR AN ENTRY RUN IN TWO FORMATS

There are two methods of performing an entry run in two formats. Refer to Figure 10-1 and note that the PROG switch has three positions. We are interested in two positions. NORMAL AND PROG REVERT.

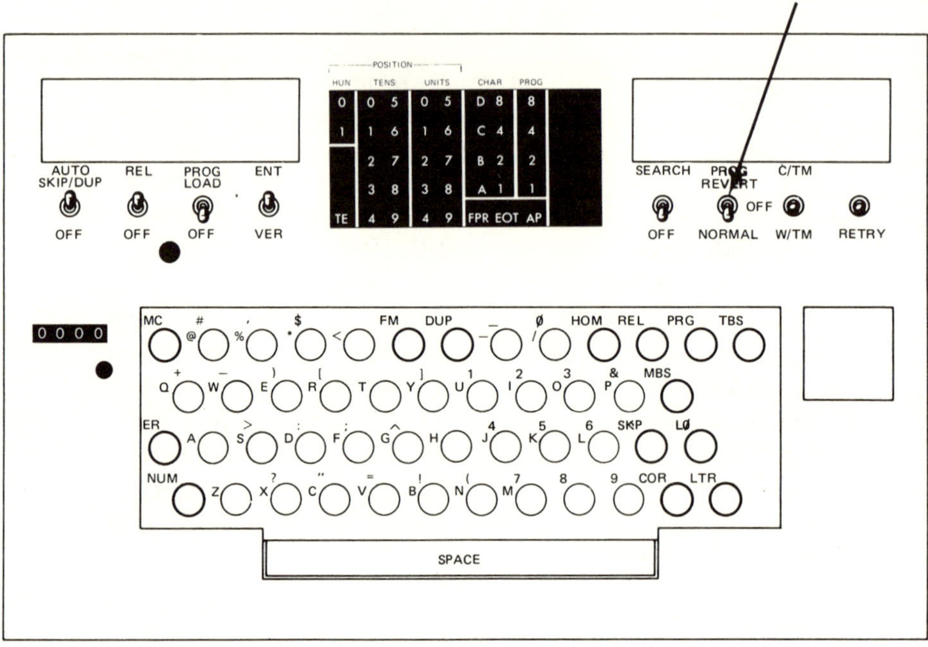

FIGURE 10-1

1) When setting the **PROG** switch to **NORMAL**, an automatic change from ALT to MAIN will not occur at the release. The program in control before the release will still be in control after data is released to the tape.

In an entry run using Format 1 and Format 2 you may SET SWITCH PROG-NORMAL and then change to the MAIN program to key a Format 1 record; change to the ALT program and key a Format 2 record.

Change back to the MAIN program and key a Format 1 record; Change to the ALT program and key a Format 2 record and so on.

To increase data entry speeds, there is a procedure to automatically change to the MAIN program.

2) Setting the **PROG** switch to **REVERT** causes a release after which the MAIN program is in control regardless of which program was in control before the release.

SET SWITCH PROG-REVERT then:

Key a Format 1 record; after it is written, manually change to the ALT program

Key a Format 2 record; after it is written an automatic change to the MAIN program occurs

Key a Format 1 record; after it is written, manually change to the ALT program

Key a Format 2 record; after it is written an automatic change to the MAIN program occurs

Exercise 2

Use the payroll source documents(pg. 118)to perform an entry run using both methods, i.e.   SET SWITCH PROG-NORMAL
SET SWITCH PROG-REVERT

Consider a situation where one or more Format 2 records follow a Format 1 record. An accounts receivable record offers a good example where Format 1 would contain customer information and each purchase is placed in a Format 2 record. The number of purchases will vary by customer. In this type of situation Format 1 is loaded into ALTERNATE memory and Format 2 is loaded into MAIN memory. Then SET SWITCH PROG-REVERT

Use the following procedures: (begin with ALTernate memory)

1) Key a Format 1 record; after it is written, an automatic change to the MAIN program occurs.

2) Key all Format 2 records. After the last Format 2 record for this customer has been written, manually change to the ALTERNATE program.

3) Key in the next Format 1 record, after it is written an automatic change to the MAIN program occurs.

4) Key in the next Format 2 records, after the last Format 2 record for this customer has been written, manually change to the ALTERNATE program, etc.

PAYROLL RECORDS

Format 1

SOC. SEC. #	NAME	ADDRESS	CITY	STATE	ZIP	MARITAL STATUS	DEP.	TYPE	NUMBER	SECURITY	ID
123-45-6789	John Smith	35 Main St.	Batavia	N.Y.	14020	M	3	04	30251	B	1

Format 2

RATE	HOURS	OVERTIME	GROSS	FICA	Y-T-D STATE	FEDERAL	VACATION PAY	HEALTH	DUES	RET.	NUMBER	BLDG.	ID
4.00	40	2	172.00				320.00	7.25	5.00	12.32	30251	AB11	2

Format 1

SOC. SEC. #	NAME	ADDRESS	CITY	STATE	ZIP	MARITAL STATUS	DEP.	TYPE	NUMBER	SECURITY	ID
063-42-9811	Bill Jones	23 Walnut St.	Buffalo	N.Y.	14240	S	0	01	11103	C	1

Format 2

RATE	HOURS	OVERTIME	GROSS	FICA	Y-T-D STATE	FEDERAL	VACATION PAY	HEALTH	DUES	RET.	NUMBER	BLDG.	ID
3.25	35		113.75					5.00	2.25	10.00	11103	B21	2

Format 1

SOC. SEC. #	NAME	ADDRESS	CITY	STATE	ZIP	MARITAL STATUS	DEP.	TYPE	NUMBER	SECURITY	ID
077-44-9999	Alice May	4413 Dwyer	Rochester	N.Y.	14240	M	2	04	67541	B	1

Format 2

RATE	HOURS	OVERTIME	GROSS	FICA	Y-T-D STATE	FEDERAL	VACATION PAY	HEALTH	DUES	RET.	NUMBER	BLDG.	ID
3.00	40		120.00					7.25	5.00	12.32	67541	C	1

Format 1

SOC. SEC. #	NAME	ADDRESS	CITY	STATE	ZIP	MARITAL STATUS	DEP.	TYPE	NUMBER	SECURITY	ID
176-33-0987	Linda Murray	23rd St. East	Buffalo	N.Y.	14240	S	0	01	54321	B	1

Format 2

RATE	HOURS	OVERTIME	GROSS	Y-T-D FICA	Y-T-D STATE	Y-T-D FEDERAL	VACATION PAY	HEALTH	DUES	RET.	NUMBER	BLDG.	ID
3.00	40		120.00					5.00	2.25	10.00	54321	B	2

Format 1

SOC. SEC. #	NAME	ADDRESS	CITY	STATE	ZIP	MARITAL STATUS	DEP.	TYPE	NUMBER	SECURITY	ID
107-46-0559	Susan Burr	2361 Forest Dr.	Batavia	N.Y.	14020	M	1	04	77777	B	1

Format 2

RATE	HOURS	OVERTIME	GROSS	Y-T-D FICA	Y-T-D STATE	Y-T-D FEDERAL	VACATION PAY	HEALTH	DUES	RET.	NUMBER	BLDG.	ID
3.25	35		113.75					7.25	5.00	12.32	77777	AC3	2

Format 1

SOC. SEC. #	NAME	ADDRESS	CITY	STATE	ZIP	MARITAL STATUS	DEP.	TYPE	NUMBER	SECURITY	ID
999-14-2202	Raymond Pier	Jefferson St.	Oakfield	N.Y.	14125	S	1	01	78901	B	1

Format 2

RATE	HOURS	OVERTIME	GROSS	Y-T-D FICA	Y-T-D STATE	Y-T-D FEDERAL	VACATION PAY	HEALTH	DUES	RET.	NUMBER	BLDG.	ID
4.25	40	5	201.88				340.00	5.00	2.25	10.00	78901	C	2

Exercise 3

Make a program planning card from the following:

FORMAT 1

Field Name	Positions	Data Type
Customer Number	1 - 5	Numeric
Customer Name	6 - 30	Alphabetic
Customer Address	31 - 50	Alphabetic
City State	51 - 70	Alphabetic
Zip	71 - 75	Numeric
Credit Rating	76 - 76	Numeric
Skip	77 - 79	Spaces
Format ID	80 - 80	Numeric

FORMAT 2

Field Name	Positions	Data Type
Customer Number	1 - 5	Auto Dup
Item Description	6 - 25	Alphabetic
Item Number	26 - 30	Numeric
Skip	31 - 40	Spaces
Quantity	41 - 43	Numeric
Price	44 - 50	Numeric
Purchase Date	51 - 58	Numeric
Skip	59 - 70	Spaces
Salesman ID	71 - 79	Alphabetic
Format ID	80 - 80	Numeric

Load Format 1 into ALTERNATE memory

Load Format 2 into MAIN memory

Using the following source documents create the accounts receivable file on tape:

A note on the PROG switch: When this switch is set to OFF your program will *not* be in control. This is a useful feature when it is desirable to enter alphabetic characters in a field defined as numeric.

Format 1

CUSTOMER NUMBER	CUSTOMER NAME	ADDRESS	CITY, STATE	ZIP CODE	CREDIT	ID
00455	Murphy Express	Dellinger Ave.	Batavia, N.Y.	14020	2	1

Format 2

DATE	ITEM DESCRIPTION	ITEM NUMBER	QUANTITY	PRICE	SALESMAN	ID
1/30/73	Chairs	30142	17	204.40	09632123	2
2/6/73	File Cabinets	70613	2	150.00	09632123	2
2/8/73	Desk	11134	1	125.00	09632123	2

Format 1

CUSTOMER NUMBER	CUSTOMER NAME	ADDRESS	CITY, STATE	ZIP CODE	CREDIT	ID
00456	Caledonia Fence	17 Pine St.	Caledonia, N.Y.	14423	1	1

Format 2

DATE	ITEM DESCRIPTION	ITEM NUMBER	QUANTITY	PRICE	SALESMAN	ID
12/5/72	150' of Wire Fence	23895	150	320.00	77324561	2
12/20/72	52 lbs. cement	00071	52	75.00	77324561	2
1/4/73	20 sq. ft. plastic	55913	20	25.60	77324561	2
1/18/73	4 gal. white paint	44435	4	32.50	77324561	2
2/8/73	8' of fine molding	22341	8	47.13	77324561	2

Format 1

CUSTOMER NUMBER	CUSTOMER NAME	ADDRESS	CITY, STATE	ZIP CODE	CREDIT	ID
30678	DeWitt Inc.	19 Harvester Pl.	Buffalo, N.Y.	14240	1	1

Format 2

DATE	ITEM DESCRIPTION	ITEM NUMBER	QUANTITY	PRICE	SALESMAN	ID
1/3/73	3" Plastic Tube	77658	10	22.00	34590838	2
1/9/73	19' Steel Frame	99999	19	189.00	34590838	2

Format 1

CUSTOMER NUMBER	CUSTOMER NAME	ADDRESS	CITY, STATE	ZIP CODE	CREDIT	ID
78650	Enterprise Corp.	341 Pine Dr.	Rochester, N.Y.	14624	2	1

Format 2

DATE	ITEM DESCRIPTION	ITEM NUMBER	QUANTITY	PRICE	SALESMAN	ID
2/13/73	2" paint brushes	55643	1	1.00	65433456	2

Format 1

CUSTOMER NUMBER	CUSTOMER NAME	ADDRESS	CITY, STATE	ZIP CODE	CREDIT	ID
54634	Miles Trucking	Thouston Dr.	Kenmore, N.Y.	14217	3	1

Format 2

DATE	ITEM DESCRIPTION	ITEM NUMBER	QUANTITY	PRICE	SALESMAN	ID
2/12/73	Swivel Chairs	89034	2	96.00	00897865	2
2/13/73	Office Desks	C6546	2	345.00	00897865	2

Chapter 11

HEADER AND TRAILER LABELS

Header and trailer labels with associated tape marks are frequently used. The format of these labels varies from installation to installation. Therefore, the following is to be considered only as a guide. Fig. 11-1 shows a typical sequence. The header label identifies the beginning of a file. It may contain:

1) The file name or number

2) The date it was created

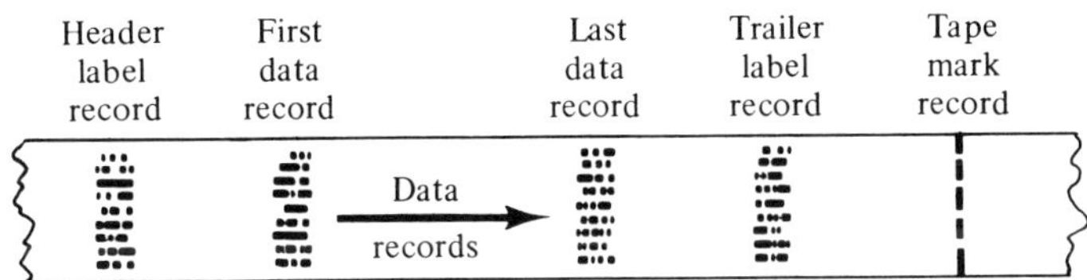

FIGURE 11-1

The trailer label identifies the end of file. It may contain:

1) A count of the records in the file

2) Totals of amounts, purchases etc.

A tape mark is a signal to the computer to stop reading records. Tape marks, therefore, are written at the end of a file. A tape mark is coded as A21 and is written by moving the TM switch to the W/TM or Write Tape Mark position, and then releasing the switch.

Note that when the tape mark has been written, the EOT indicator will go ON and the ERROR light will flash. To clear a tape mark, move the TM switch to the C/TM or Clear Tape Mark position and then release it. This is important when writing several batches of records on tape since you will be unable to add records to a file if a tape mark has been read into data memory by the data recorder.

In the verification run, (page 95) the tape mark has been cleared by moving the TM switch to the C/TM position. If a tape mark has been written in an entry run or read in a verification run and you must add records to the file, move the TM switch to the C/TM position.

Exercise 1

You are to create a header and trailer label for the billing file, Figure 9-2. (Do not use a Program Planning Card.)

To enter the header label key:

> BILLING TAPE in positions 1-12
> Skip positions 13-70
> Today's date in positions 71-78
> Skip position 79
> H in position 80

To enter the trailer label enter:

> END BILL FILE in positions 1-13
> Skip positions 14-60
> Number of records in file, positions 61-62
> Skip positions 63-70

*The total purchase amount 0000000 in positions 71-77
Skip positions 78-79
T in position 80

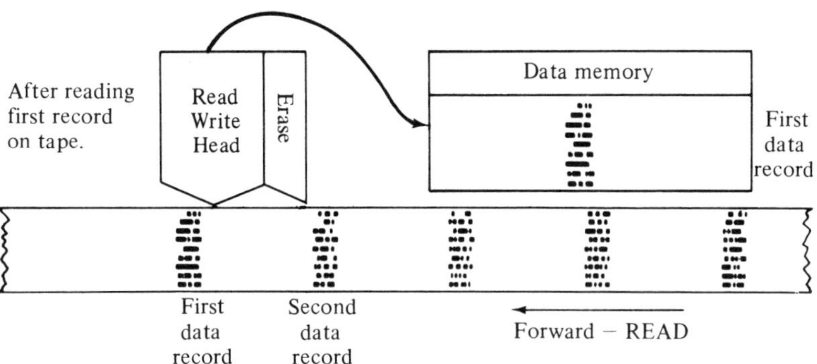

FIGURE 11-2

Re-key Figure 9-2 using the header and trailer records given in this exercise and enter the tape mark. It is also possible to add forgotten header and trailer records.

The trailer record also can be added using the SEARCH procedures on page 110 omitting steps 13, 14, 15, and 16. After step 12 perform the following additional steps:

17)   ER key

18)   Verify the tape mark by depressing the RETRY switch

19)   Move the TM switch to C/TM to clear the tape mark, then depress the ER key

20)   SET S-OFF

21)   To erase the tape mark, depress the ER/TBS keys before the entry operation

22)   Add the trailer record

23)   Add a tape mark after the trailer record.

The header record can also be added during a verification run. If after the first record has been read into data memory, it is found *not* to be a header label (Figure 11-2) the header label must be added. In this position a header label would normally have been read. Of course, it cannot be verified if it has

*For the computer to calculate.

not yet been written. In order to get the header label on tape depress the ER/TBS keys. To enter the header label the correction procedure for ER/FM or ER/COR should be used.

    After re-verification, the header label will be found in front of the first data record as shown in Figure 11-3.

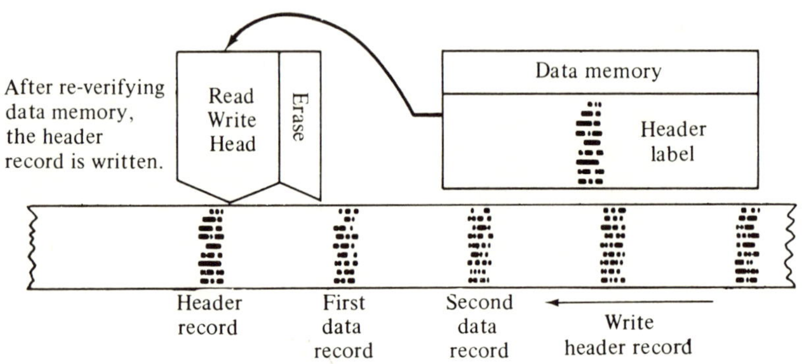

FIGURE 11-3

Exercise 2

Add your own header and trailer labels on tape 2, Chapter 7, exercise 1.

Exercise 3

Add the following employees to the payroll records in exercise 2, page 119.

PAYROLL RECORD

Format 1

SOC. SEC. #	NAME	ADDRESS	CITY	STATE	ZIP	MARITAL STATUS	DEP.	TYPE	NUMBER	SECURITY	ID
015-76-0539	Joseph Adams	4 Cherry St.	Batavia	N.Y.	14020	S	1	01	00002	D	1

Format 2

RATE	HOURS	OVERTIME	GROSS	Y-T-D FICA	STATE	FEDERAL	VACATION PAY	HEALTH	DUES	RET.	NUMBER	BLDG.	ID
5.50	40	8	286.00				220.00	5.00	2.25	10.00	00002	D1	2

Format 1

SOC. SEC. #	NAME	ADDRESS	CITY	STATE	ZIP	MARITAL STATUS	DEP.	TYPE	NUMBER	SECURITY	ID
063-42-9876	Homer Wells	Longhorn Dr.	Depew	N.Y.	14043	S	0	01	34567	C	1

Format 2

RATE	HOURS	OVERTIME	GROSS	Y-T-D FICA	STATE	FEDERAL	VACATION PAY	HEALTH	DUES	RET.	NUMBER	BLDG.	ID
4.00	40		160.00				160.00	5.00	2.25	10.00	34567	D1	2

Chapter 12

OPERATION HINTS

CORRECTING A MULTI-CODED CHARACTER DURING A VERIFICATION RUN

Multi-coded characters cannot be corrected in the same manner that a standard keyboard character can because standard multi-coded characters require two or more depressions of the COR key.

The following serves as an example:

Change the character CB1 to C41

1) Hold down the ER/MC keys

2) Depress COR, then C

3) Depress COR, then 4

4) Depress COR, then 1

Release the ER/MC keys.

After reverification, C41 is written to tape.

CORRECTING AN AUTO DUP ERROR IN THE SAME FIELD FOR MANY RECORDS.

Instead of correcting each duplicate field when verifying all records, it is faster to first correct the duplicate fields only. Then resume normal verification.

This can be accomplished by loading, through the keyboard, a program which will automatically skip all positions in a record *except* those in the field to be corrected. This field should be programmed as a manual entry field in alphabetic or numeric mode depending on the data items. Then SET SWITCH M-VER and read and verify the next record with AS/D-ON

make the required correction using the ER/COR keys

continue verifying and correcting the same field

rewind the tape

reload the original program

initiate a search for the first record that contained the error in the auto dup field

continue verifying the remaining records in the file

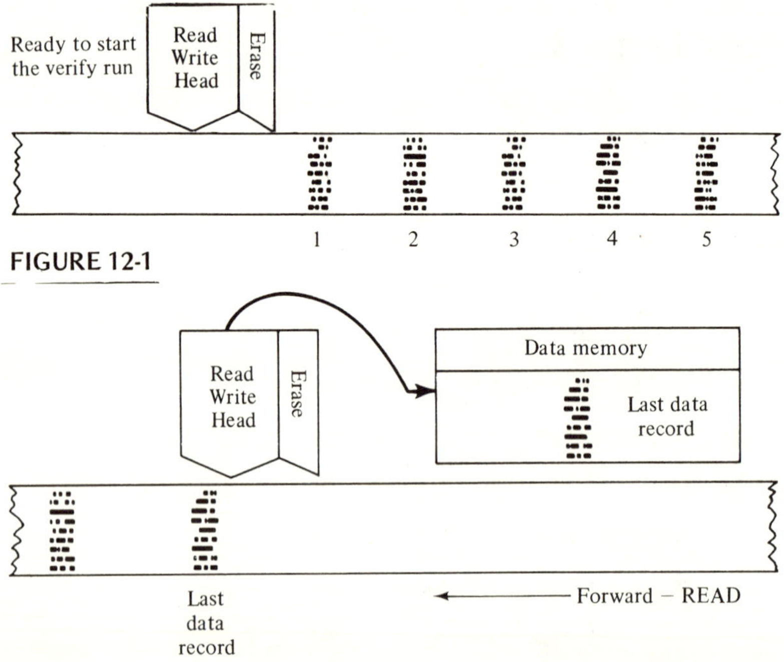

FIGURE 12-1

FIGURE 12-2

Verify the last record and prepare the machine for an entry run. Key in the first data record to be added to the file. The new record will be written immediately after the last old record and the tape mark record (if any) will be erased. This is shown in Figure 12-3.

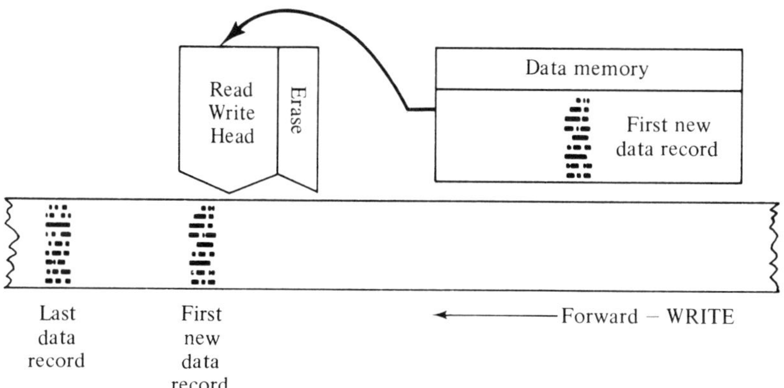

FIGURE 12-3

ADDING NEW RECORDS TO A FILE

The procedure to do this is similar to adding new records after a verification run. However, the presence or absence of a tape mark is significant.

A) *In the absence of a tape mark*

Initiate a search for the last record. When it is found, it will be to the left of the read/write head. (Figure 12-4). At this time prepare the machine for an entry run. Keying in the first record places it directly after the last data record on the old file. Continue the entry run.

B) *With a tape mark present*

Initiate a search for the tape mark. When the search is completed, the tape mark will be to the left of the read/write head. Depress the TBS (Tape Back Space key) in order to move the tape mark to the right of the erase head and clear the tape mark in memory by depressing the C/TM switch (See page 124.) Refer to Figure 12-5. Prepare the data recorder for an entry run. After keying in the first of the new records the tape will move forward erasing the tape mark (Figure 12-6) and the first new record will be placed directly after the last old record. Continue entering new records. If you forget to depress the TBS key, the erase head will not be able to remove the tape mark. The result will be two files of records separated by a tape mark. See Figure 12-7. When this tape is submitted for processing by the computer the tape mark will cause processing to stop. The new records will not be read by the computer.

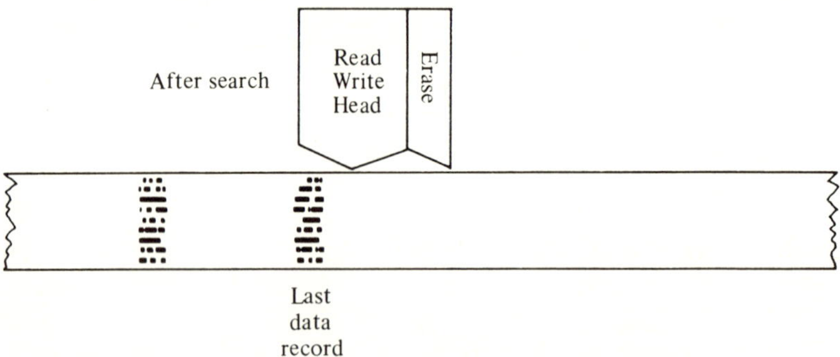

FIGURE 12-4

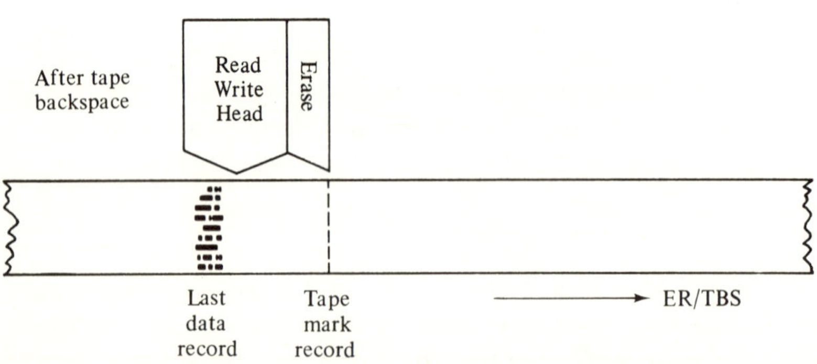

FIGURE 12-5

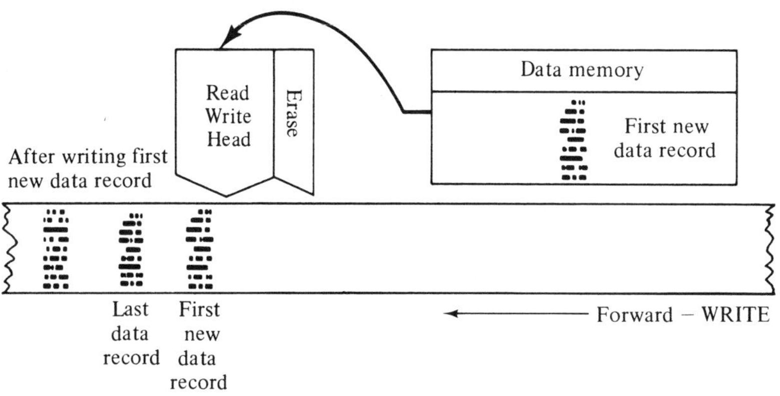

FIGURE 12-6

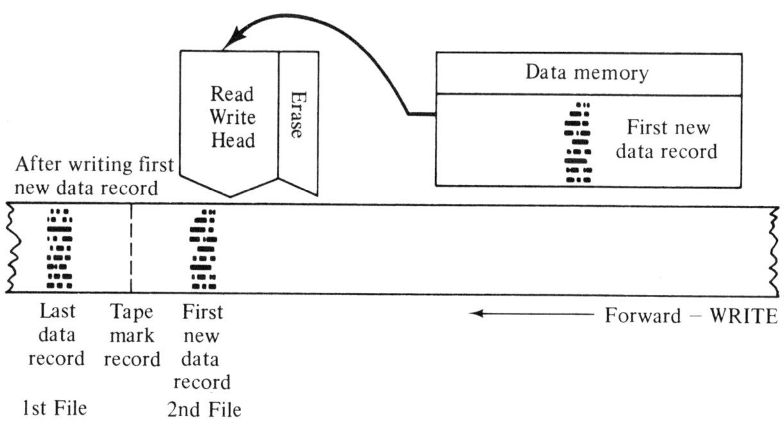

FIGURE 12-7

CODING A RECORD FOR COMPUTER SELECTION

Duplicate or unwanted records may be deleted during computer processing. The following procedures should be followed.

Instructions   *Explanation*

1) SET SWITCHES
      AS/ — OFF   prevent auto skip/dup
        R — REL   to permit release

PL — OFF	not loading a program
M — VER	to verify
S — OFF	not searching
P — as required	

2) ER/HOM — to begin at position 001

3) Verify characters — to advance to position to be altered

4) Enter the *delete* characters after setting M-ENT or using the ER/COR keys — this character or characters and the positions they reside in *must* be specified by a supervisor or computer programmer

5) ER/HOM — to return to position 001

6) Re-verify the entire record — to be certain that the delete characters are correctly entered

AFTER RELEASE OCCURS THE DELETE CHARACTERS ARE ON TAPE

7) Change SWITCHES AS/D as required

8) REL key — to read the next data record into memory

CONTINUE ON WITH THE RUN

DELETING A RECORD
DURING A VERIFICATION RUN

Duplicated records may be removed during a verification run. We will use the keyboard switch marked REC DEL shown in Fig. 12-8. To remove an unwanted record from the tape file, do the following:

Hold down the ER key

Move the switch to REC DEL and release it

Release the ER key

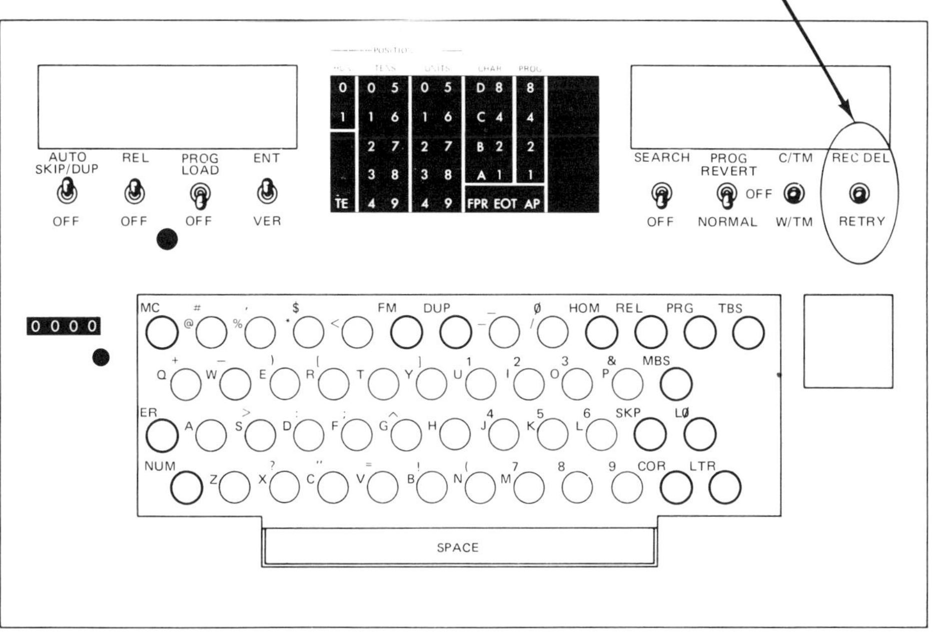

FIGURE 12-8

This procedure causes the unwanted record to be erased from the tape and the operator may continue with the verification run.

VERIFYING THE LAST RECORD WRITTEN DURING AN ENTRY RUN

To determine the last record written in order to continue a run, the last record must be read. Since this record is just to the left of the read/write head:

SET SWITCH M-VER

Depress the RETRY switch to backspace the tape one record length. The tape will next move forward and read the desired record into data memory. See Fig. 12-9.

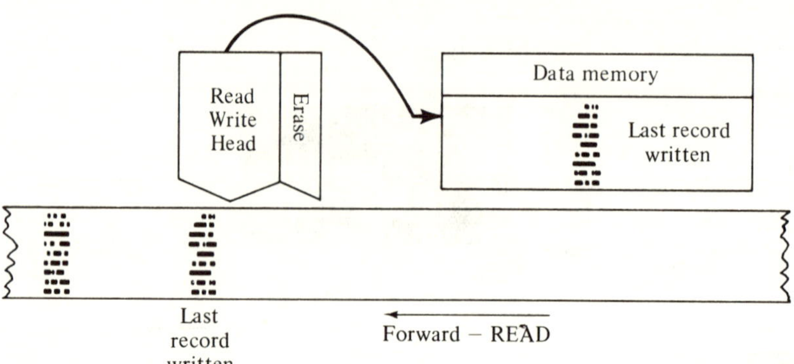

FIGURE 12-9

With the last record now in data memory you can verify it or read it out from the data memory display lamps 1 position at a time.

DO THE FOLLOWING FOR AN ENTRY RUN ONLY: VERIFY THE LAST RECORD WRITTEN.

Instructions	*Explanation*
1) SET SWITCHES	
AS/D – OFF	prevent auto skip/dup
R – REL	permit release
PL – OFF	not loading a program
M – VER	to read a record from tape
S – OFF	not searching
P – as required	
2) Depress the RETRY switch	to back up one record length and read the last record into data memory
3) Change SWITCH R-OFF	to prevent release (there are no additional records on tape)
4) Verify entire record using CHAR display and the EB CDIC code	

5) Change SWITCHES

M – ENT	to continue the entry run
R – REL	to permit release
AS/D – ON	to permit auto skip/dup

6) ER/HOM   to begin from position 001

Continue with the entry run adding new records or verifying records that have been previously added to the file.

Chapter 13

OTHER KEYBOARD DATA ENTRY DEVICES

There are many types of keyboard devices used to enter data into a computer system, i.e., keyboard terminals, which use cathode ray tubes called CRTs, and so on. In this chapter, we will only be concerned with those devices that are used to prepare large volumes of records for processing by a computer.

THE KEYPUNCH

The keypunch stores data in the form of punched holes on cards. A typical keypunch is shown in Fig. 13-1.

This type of data entry device has been in use since the 1890 census. However, recent trends in electronic data entry devices such as the 1100 and 6400 Family of Data Recorders of Mohawk Data Sciences Corp. and the Inforex System have made great improvements over the punched card method of data entry.

FIGURE 13-1

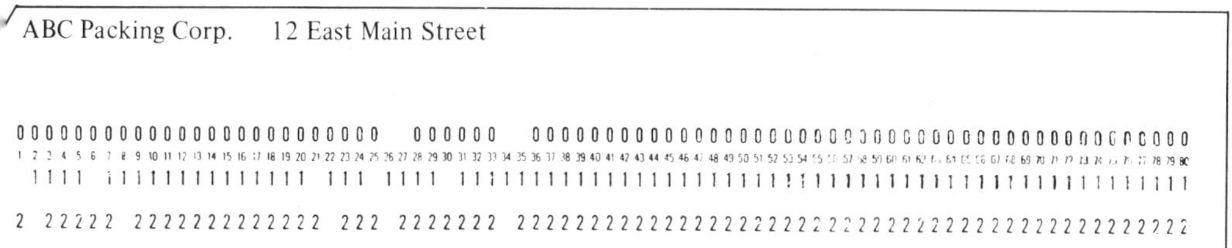

ABC Packing Corp.   12 East Main Street

FIGURE 13-2

Punched cards (Fig. 13-2) have some disadvantages:

1. Punched cards can only store 80 characters of informa-
    tion on a surface area 7 3/8" by 3¼". This means more

storage space is required for cards than for tape or disk records.

2. An error on a card requires that an entirely new card be rekeypunched.

3. Card input to the computers central processing unit is slow compared to data transmission speeds for tape and disk. The fastest punch card reader can read 2,000 cards or 160,000 characters per minute. Information on magnetic tape can be read at 1.3 million characters per minute.

4. Worn or damaged cards usually cause time-consuming card jams on the computer's card readers which slow down production runs.

FIGURE 13-3   courtesy Honeywell Information Systems, Inc.

HONEYWELL KEYTAPE DEVICE

A machine similar to the Mohawk Data Recorder is the Honeywell Keytape Device. It is shown in Fig. 13-3.

One basic difference between the Mohawk and Honeywell machines is that the Mohawk machine feeds the tape into a bin while the Honeywell machine winds the tape reel to reel. Both machines are similar, but more complex than the keypunch.

MAGNETIC DATA INSCRIBER

The IBM 50 Magnetic Data Inscriber (Fig. 13-4) contains a keyboard similar to the keypunch (Fig. 13-1). Each tape is housed in a self-contained cartridge and each 100 ft. tape reel may contain 23,000 characters. The use of a self-contained

FIGURE 13-4

cartridge makes tape handling and threading unnecessary for the operator. The operator merely inserts the cartridge in its proper position and selects the desired mode of operation—writing, verifying or reading. Tape records move in synchronization with the control unit, much like the movement of the card on the keypunch.

INFOREX

FIGURE 13-5

Keyboard & Tape Units

The Inforex system includes keyboard disc and tape units and like the data recorder, was developed because of the need for input faster than cards.

FIGURE 13-6

Data from source documents is keyed onto a disc located behind the control unit. The disc can contain up to 18,000 records of 125 characters in length. The control unit places input under the control of the operator much like the programs written for the data recorder and like the control unit of the data recorder, the Inforex control unit diagnoses errors, locking out the keyboard until previous data entry errors are corrected. The CRT displays a full record on its screen making possible sight verification. (See Fig. 13-5)

Data transfer from disc to tape (Fig. 13-6) is permitted by the operator when a file of records is corrected and entered on a disc. Header and trailer records that are used for several jobs may be stored on disc by the operator and "called" into a file of records as appropriate.

APPENDIX A

This appendix contains three types of keying drills for:

1)   Numeric Characters

2)   Alphabetic Characters

3)   Special Characters

These exercises are designed to familiarize the student with the keyboard and should be used as drills to increase speed and accuracy of keying.

Drills 1, 2 and 3 contain 800 characters or 80 keying strokes per line for 10 lines (not including spaces) and may be used with the chart below to approximately measure your speed.

SPEED CHART

Time for Drill	Key Strokes Per Hour	Key Strokes Per minute
48 minutes	1000	16.7
24	2000	33.3
16	3000	50.0
12	4000	66.7
8	6000	100.0
6	8000	133.3
4.8	10000	166.7
4	12000	200.0

Numeric Drills

0100 0101 0102 0103 0104 0105 0106 0107 0108 0109 0901 0801 0701 0601 0501 0401 0301 0201 0101 0102
0201 0213 0226 0238 0250 0272 0284 0296 0211 0212 0213 0214 0215 0216 0217 0218 0219 0220 0221 0222
0301 0312 0324 0336 0348 0360 0372 0384 0396 0369 0381 0393 0313 0323 0324 0325 0326 0327 0328 0329
0401 1414 1416 1418 1420 1422 1424 1426 1428 1430 1432 1434 1436 1438 1440 1442 1444 1446 1448 1450
0501 1515 1517 1519 1521 1523 1525 1527 1529 1531 1533 1535 1537 1539 1541 1543 1545 1547 1549 1551
0601 1616 1618 1620 1622 1624 1626 1628 1630 1632 1634 1636 1638 1640 1642 1644 1646 1648 1650 1652
0701 0707 0713 0719 0725 0731 0737 0743 0749 0755 0761 0767 0773 0779 0785 0791 0797 0779 0719 0758
0801 1818 1820 1822 1823 1824 1826 1828 1830 1832 1834 1836 1818 1820 1822 1824 1826 1828 1830 1832
0901 0906 0911 0916 0921 0926 0931 0937 0941 0946 0951 0956 0961 0967 0972 0977 0982 0987 0992 0997
0001 0002 0003 0004 0005 0006 0007 0008 0009 0010 0011 0012 0013 0014 0015 0016 0017 0018 0019 0020

Drill

ABAC ABBA BAAB CABB BACC CACA BABA AABC ABAA BABA CABA AABB BBAA CCAB BBCA ABCA ABCB CCBA CBCB CCBA
DACA DABA DBAC DCAB ADAB ADAC DCBA DCBC CBDA CCDA DBAC DDAB DDAA DDAC DDCA DDBA DABA BADC CADD BADA
EDAC EDCB EBDI EDIC EEDA EEDB EEDC EDEC EDEB EDEA EBEE EDEE DDEA EBED DDDE EDCA ADCE BACE BADE DAEE
FACE FAAC FBCA BFAC DBFA FECA FEBA BEFA DEFB EDFA FEDA FDEA FDDA FEEC FEED EEFA AAFA ABFA DBFA FBFA
FBFF FCFF FDAF AACF FDAF CCCF ABAF FAFF FABF GABF GBDF BACF FAFB BAFB CABF DAAF DAAF BABF FAFA BAFA
DAFA CAFA DAFF DABF FBBF GFBA GDCA GGAG GFGF GFFA GFDE GFED FGDE FDEG DEEG DEFG DEEG AFFG DFFG FBGG
HFGA HGFE EFGH FEGH GHDE HABC AHAC BHAD DEGH CDGH ABDH ACHE HEAD HICH ICHA IBHD CHAB GHDE IFGH FGHI
IIGH IEEI HIHH HIGH IIED JICJ FGHJ GHIJ JIHJ GIHJ HIJJ IHJJ IJHJ HIJK KJIH JKIH JJIH IHIJ HIJJ IJJK
HIJK KIKK HIJK KDEG IJKL HIJG LOIC KLIK JKIK LIJK LKIJ KIJL JLKI JJJK KJJJ LKJL IKKL KIIL IKLL JKLM
MLJK JJML JMMJ KMMK KMKM MFJL NOMN MNON NOMM MONN MONO OMMO NNJN NOMO MNOO ONNO ONON NONO OOON NOOO

DRILL

PPPP POOH OOOP PHJI HIPH POHJ OPPO HIJP IPIJ QUOP QUIP POQU UQIP POQU QQQP PQQQ RPQR RRIP SPUR PURS
JKPR SRRS RSSR USSR RUSS FRUS SURF STUF TUFF TURF SITS FSTR RUTT UTTU TUUT UTUU STUT STUV VUST EVER
IVYR EVEN EVVV ERVE SERV CVJK JKVV SKVM SKYV VERV REVE GREV VRFF WEVE EWHE TWIN SWEE WEST WEWR SEEW
SNOW NOWS REWH WHIT WWHE WHEN WWWH XWXW WXWX WXXW WXWX XWWX WHWX WHXX SXYH SWXS JUJW JUJX HJXJ YXXY
YXXX XYXY XYYY JUJX JUJY YJUJ XHXJ XJHJ WAXY YYAM MAYY XYYX WXXX XYXY YARD TRYY JOYS ZEBR ZZZZ AZAZ
PZAX ZZPZ XYZX JUYZ ZONE SIZZ XYZY YWXZ WXYZ ZZZO ZERO ZXZX PZAZ VRXW ZQRZ RSTZ YXWZ PMNZ ZEST ZZOE
ABCD EFGH IJKL MNOP QRST UVWX YZAB CDEF GHIJ KLMN OPQR STUV WXYZ AABB CCDD EEFF GGHH IIJJ KKLL MMNN
OOPP QQRR SSTT UUVV WWXX YYZZ ABAC ACAB VXYZ WXYZ MNOP TRYS BLPM YNGJ LWPG BTNO KMON SWIX ZTYM INRS
ASPX DWON GHXY JUJJ PJUJ RSTY RUST FREE PONY QUIP SWAY EXIT FIXS MANY LOVE CROP DROP SCAT GONE SOME
OLEO SHOO ZERO LOCO COMA CALA IOTA ILIA LAMA HULA GALA OLLA RAJA SOTA CRIB CURB PLEB SWAB GAMB KERB

STOB TOMB VERB SCAB SHEA SODA ROTA PUMA PICA SWOB KNOB LIMB GULF DEAF CALF BEEF SELF PUFF RUFF DUFF
KEEF PELF SERV ABRI AGNI ASCI GYRI KAKI KEPI LOCI NIDI NISI PALI RAGI SOLI TAXI YOGI ALSO BOLO COCO
LOTO GALO HERO KINO OLEO PEPO TARO TIRO TYRO UNDO ZERO BABU BEAU HABU IGLU JUJU KUDU MENU LIEU THOU
THRU TOLU UNAU ZEBU BICE ECAD GAMB SKEG SLUB ZOON SOJA EMEU FUZE MAZE QUIZ SOON SIZZ TZAR ZEAL ZANY
COXY FRIZ ZEIN ZEST HAZY ZOIC OYEZ OOZY ZALA WHIZ JAZZ BUZZ CZAR ADZE AZYM ZINC ZOON ZOOM ZETA RAZE
IBEX FLUX ILEX IXIA JINX FLEX FLAX FOXY LYNX AXLE EXIT AXIX APEX MOXA PIXY ONYX TEXT TAXI NEXT HOAX
TAXY CRUX EAUX FOXY IBEX ILEX IXIA MINX OXIM ABED BADE BEAD ACHE EACH ACRES CARES RACES SCARE AIDS
DAIS SAID ALEX SALE SEAL AMEN MANE MEAN NAME AMEND MANED NAMED ANGEL ANGLE GLEAN ARID RAID ARIL
LAIR LIAR RAIL ARISE RAISE ASCOT COAST ASIDE IDEAS ASTER RATES STARE TARES TEARS ASTIR STAIR BALES
BLASE SABLE BARED BEARD BREAD BELOW BOWEL ELBOW BLEATING TANGIBLE BLEATS STABLE TABLES BRAID RABID

BRIEF FIBER BROWSE BOWERS CAPERS CRAPES PACERS SCRAPE RECAPS SPACER CAPES PACES SPACE SCAPE CARET
CATER CRATE TRACE CARTEL CLARET CAUSE SAUCE CHASTE CHEATS SCATHE CHEATER TEACHER CITED EDICT CLEAT
ECLAT COIL LOCI COINS ICONS SCION SONIC CORSET SECTOR CREDIT DIRECT CRISP SCRIP DALE DEAL LADE
LEAD DARE DEAR READ DANGER GANDER GARDEN RANGED DEALER LEADER REDEAL DENIED INDEED DESIGN SIGNED
SINGED DETAIL DILATE TAILED DIET EDIT TIDE TIED DRAWS SWARD WARDS DRAPES PARSED SPADER SPARED
SPREAD EARTH HATER HEART EAST EATS ETAS SATE SEAT SETA ELAPSE PLEASE EMIT MITE TIME ITEMS ENTRAP
PARENT ERRING RINGER ESTER STEER TREES ETHER THERE THREE FARES FEARS SAFER FASTER STRAFE FIELD
FILED FLIED FILE LIFE LIEF FILER FLIER RIFLE LIFER FINGER FRINGE GARNETS STRANGE GIRTH RIGHT GLARE
LAGER LARGE REGAL GNAT TANG RRANITE TEARING GROAN ORANG HARES HEARS SHARE SHEAR HEWN WHEN HINGES
NEIGHS HOES SHOE HOSE HORSE HOSER SHORE INERT INTER NITER NITRE TRINE INKS KINS SINK SKIN INSET

ZIPCODE DRILL

01536 01887 01259 01771 02093 02380 02130 14058 14020 14428 22304 22740 22976 24616 23480 25563
37160 37152 37375 37689 37872 37179 37893 37881 37886 37602 37851 38070 38077 37860 37376 37379
48812 48217 48726 48809 48110 48808 48019 49908 49711 49306 49619 49807 49303 49825 49729 49925
56732 56256 55115 56001 56657 56258 55752 55943 55335 55111 55020 56442 55725 56401 55909 55721
68811 68964 68860 68658 68005 68931 69336 68014 69127 68823 68365 64441 65470 63135 65717 64449
74634 74733 74860 74857 74734 75901 76858 79252 77871 77458 79383 76944 79701 76520 77360 78658
80026 81143 81152 85326 86431 85612 85324 85614 85621 85344 85616 85331 86503 85901 85257 85542
99658 99773 99640 99753 99676 99688 97429 97114 97301 97825 97349 97857 97635 97043 97739 97866
35804 90052 48502 14603 14020 78710 27260 59101 62521 47808 91408 89501 23369 43216 53703 13503
87544 10023 88354 68718 68728 69334 59354 87743 28208 27817 27263 99732 58417 27592 41565 71347

DRILL

TUCSON FREMONT LANSING MUSKEGON PONTIAC SPRINGFIELD YOUNGSTOWN MILWAUKEE NEWPORT WATERBURY YORK
FLINT CLEVELAND AKRON SEATTLE EVANSTON RENO WILMINGTON POMONA RICHMOND SANTA BARBARA TULSA ERIE
TROY YONKERS FLUSHING BUFFALO ROCHESTER BATAVIA TAMPA HOLLYWOOD SAVANNAH ANN ARBOR WORCHESTER
JACKSON LINCOLN OMAHA EUGENE SALEM BETHLEHEM OGDEN AUSTIN ABILENE AMRILLO CHARLESTON PITTSBURGH
DECATUR BOISE CHICAGO DETROIT KALAMAZOO SAGINAW LOWELL ALTO REDWOOD SACRAMENTO STAMFORD CAMDEN
ROCK GLEN WARSAW FILLMORE CHILI SPRINGVILLE CAMPBELL ELMIRA CORNING CORFU EAST PEMBROKE ELMWOOD
PERRY PAVILION ELBA BYRON DALE SANDUSKY SCIO BELFAST WELLSVILLE FREDONIA VARYBURG WEBSTER UNION
ALRED ALMOND FAYETTEVILLE ARCADE CANISTEO CANEADA CANANDAIGUA ALDEN ALBION MEDINA WYOMING RYE
ALBANY UTICA BUFFALO LACKAWANNA DEPEW EDEN CORTLAND CHURCHVILLE ATTICA ALEXANDER DUNDEE IRVING

IRONDEQUOIT HAWTHORNE HONEOYE KINFARON JOHNSTOWN ORISKANY EDMESTON SCHENECTADY STRYKERVILLE

ANN ARBOR GRAND RAPIDS BIRMINGHAM SPRINGFIELD NEWPORT WATERLOO ORLANDO JACKSONVILLE BRISTOL
TOPEKA SIOUX CITY DAVENPORT PENSACOLA GLENDALE SAN JOSE ALAMEDA LOUISVILLE LAUREL CORTLAND TROY
RICHMOND COLUMBUS HARTFORD SKANEATELES SODUS STRATFORD STRYKERSVILLE TRANSITOWN GREECE GENEVA
ELLENVILLE CHARLOTTE CLYDE COBLESKILL COLLINS CANISTEO JAMESTOWN BELMONT CHEEKTOWAGA CLARENCE
DANSVILLE GAINESVILLE HOLLAND PENN YAN JAMAICA MOUNT MORRIS NEWARK NORTHTOWN NIAGARA FALLS HUNT
WASHINGTON BURBANK LYNN FRESNO INGLEWOOD BRIDGEPORT COVINGTON ROCKFORD MACON CLEARWATER SEATTLE
FLINT DEARBORN PONTIAC ELIZABETH ORANGE RIDGEWOOD RUTHERFORD ALBUQUERQUE ELMIRA RALEIGH EUGENE
PORTLAND ALLENTOWN LANCASTER PHILADELPHIA READING YORK COLUMBIA GREENVILLE SIOUX FALLS RICHMOND
NASHVILLE LYNCHBURG ROANOAK PORTSMOUTH VIRGINIA BEACH GREEN BAY AURORA JOLIET GARY ATLANTIC CITY
EL PASO STATEN ISLAND NEW YORK CITY PEORIA INDIANAPOLIS LAFAYETTE SOUTH BEND TORRANCE LAKELAND

DRILL

```
AABB   ABAB   CEDA   BEDA   BADE   DEBA   DABB   EBDA   EDAB   FABC   BAFC   EFAC   CFEA   GHAD   GBAE   DCFE   GADE   HDAB   FGCE   FGHD
GDEF   AECH   GFED   ADGH   IFGH   FEDA   HECD   IHFG   HIJD   AIIC   CDEI   JFGI   JIJG   GJIJ   JIJG   HJIF   KJIH   GHIJ   KJII   GHJI
KJFE   EHJK   HJKI   LIJK   GHLK   MLJG   MMLF   ALMN   MNON   NOMN   DRMN   MNOD   ACEN   NMOB   BNMO   PDEB   KNAD   IJUN   QCOE   RQBM
QUIP   QUBM   RTSJ   UJIC   SRQU   RSJK   TSTJ   JUST   UGHS   VEST   WVST   JIVW   XJWV   VWUJ   XYZJ   UIXY   YXTE   ZEOR   ZEOW   WZBV
THROW   WORTH   WROTH   WIDER   WEIRD   OUGHT   NETS   TENS   SENT   ORTS   ROTS   SORT   TORS   PEST   PETS   STEP   PORES   POSER
PROSE   POINTER   PROTEIN   TROPINE   PASTE   PATES   SPATE   TAPES   RATS   STAR   TARS   RELATING   TRIANGLE   RESERVE
SEVERER   REVERSE   SAINT   SATIN   STAIN   SHEET   THESE   SLATE   STAKE   STEAK   TAKES   TEAKS   MASON   MOANS   LACES   SCALE
JERKY   JITTER   DISJECT   ADJUNCT   ADJOIN   ADJUST   ACQUIT   BISQUE   LIQUOR   INQUIRE   SQUIRT   REQUITE   SQUEEZE   QUIT
```

```
@#$%  &*(  )+=  :".?  ,./;  []@#  #$%  &=%*  &=%*  #$%@  +":?  .+,.  ?'&=  %$*(  )_@#  $%[  @#$$  %[&*
#$%!  @#$%  &*()  +-":  ?.,"  ,./  :"+_  []@#  #$%<  *&$>  @#()  #$%*  @#$%  :",.  ?.,"  :'!.  :")*
[@#$  %=&*  ()-+  -)(*  &Λ%$  @[#$  %!&*  ()_+  <":?  ,.;  ?.,"  ;'/.  +_)(  *&>%  @#$%  =&*(  _+-)
.?:"  =+_  %Λ&*  $%#$  @#()  *&!%  +<":  ?.,"  @#$%  <&*(  )_+=  ":,.  ?":=  )(*&  [@#$  $%>&  *(*%
[[[[  @@@@  ####  $$$$  %%%%  <<<<  &&&&  ****  ((((  ))))  -<->  ----  ++++  >>>>  """"  ''''  ****
,,,,  ....  $$$$  ////  """"  ''''  ::::  ;;;;  !!!!  ++++  -!-!  ****  %%%%  $$$$  ####  @@@@  ====
[@#$  %!&*  *()-  +<"=  ,.?,  .?:"  *>&%  @@#$.  %%=&  &&&*  -'&*  @@@@  $$##  %%!!  [[[[  ]]]#  ++++
[[@@  ##$$  %%ΛΛ  &&**  (())  ++""  ::??  ,,++  ))((  **&&  ΛΛ%%  $$##  @@[[  ]]@@  //.,  '''"  *&≈%
[@#$  %>&*  ()_+  ":,.  ?.,"  ++++  ))))  ((((  ****  &&&&  !!!!  %%%%  &&&&  ####  @@@@  [[[  ]]]]
++++  ----  ))**  (*&Λ  %$#@  [@#$  %!&*  &*()  ++++  ::::  ''''  """"  ////  ??//  ,.?/  (*&>  ####
```

SUPPLEMENTAL ALPHABETIC DRILLS

aaa abc all at away able away absent adverb adsorb aplomb affix aerie afflict aide aid alcove adjoins
bbb bel bet boa bog bid bit beta bide bind brad brag braid brain blue blare bomb boot bonus benzoline
ccc cab cap call camp clinic clique compel conjure connect condemn continent contralto constrain come
ddd den dhu date dash data devil dialog deuce denial destroy describe diagnosis diameter diplomat dog
eee eon erg esne ergo erect exotic erasure evolution exposure explosion exertion exhalant explore ewe
fff fa fag fable fade fain fault farina farrier festival feverish flaxseed flamingos flippant frizzle
ggg go gad gap gash gauge gerkin gourmet giraffes graceful gristmill grotesque gymnasium gyrate guava
hhh hat hash helm hewn history horseman hyacinth hygienist hyperbole humorists hypnotism hyphenize
iii it ice icy idea imid imbue immit impact impulse incisor innovate inoxidize insertion iodine ivory
jjj jo jot jest jowl junk jump jitter joggle justice juvenile junket jealousy johnnycake jonquil jig
kkk ka kid kip keel kilt knelt kazoo kimono kitchen knobby kohlrabi kumquat kerosene kangaroo kinship
lll la lag lad lair lark lanky lathe launch liberal ligament licorice limpid luminous ludicrous lucky
mmm ma map mast mail magic maize master mauve melody maximize melodrama messenger moccasin monologues
nnn no nod norm north nozle neutral navigate negotiate normalize nutriment nuzzle numbskull nostalgic
ooo on obi oval oboe olive omnibus ordinary osmosis originate oxidation oyster obsession operetta ora

ppp pa pep park pert pesky pharmacy psychology pneumonia polygonal pompadour proximate pulmonary post
qqq qu qua quip quits query quality quaff quagmire quizzical quinine quintette quotation quotient qua
rrr re rye roe rule royal resin resist rubbery ruminate rummage rutabaga rubbish rubberize rialto ret
sss si sky she scare scowl scrimp seldom semester separate serenity sextuplet sympathy symphony style
ttt to two the twin twist twitch tactic terror thither thorough throttle throaxes thyroid tourist top
uuu up use urn undo unveil umpire umbrella ukulele ungulate unnatural upholster unusual untrue urgent
vvv vie via veto vine view vigor vinyl virtu vitamin voiceless voodoo vouch volume vindicate vacation
www we won west wage walk waltz walnut weigh whistle whither wigwam willowish windsock wondrous world
xxx xyst xylic xiphoid xylem xebec
yyy yak yells yoga yotee yoghurt youngster youthful yonder yodel yellowish yachtsman yardarm yardarm
zzz zip zinc zest zebu zebra zero zany zealot zebroid zeroes zipper zircon zoologist zoology zoom

152

Alphabetic Drills

Adams Avery Aster Betts Boyle Bumps Cain Clute Conger Davis Dery Devoe Earle Ecker Edson Ford Fryes
Flynn Fisher Greer Gillard George Gray Harris Harter Harvey Havens Ingles Isaac Ivers Jensen Jaszko
Jones Jordon Keller Kilner King Klahn Landers Leaton Lewis Little Mager Magee Meyer Morse Noel Noah
Nugent Nutting Osborn Owen Oxcencis Parker Patterson Paul Quaker Radley Raymond Robins Root Salway
Sargent Sanders Schmidt Selden Taylor Terry Thompson Tootell Townsend Turner Upson Valle Viele Volz
Wicks Whyman Wilcox Wilkes Williams Wilson Wood Worthington Wright Yates Younkmann Zehler Zorn Zito
Brown Bennet Warren Philips Smith Jones Miller Reynolds Youngers Fuller Cramer Wagner Tooley Pratt
Preston Wolff Arnold Baker Harper Clark Goodman Mullins Parks Peters Benton Nichols Meisner Strollo
Thomas Sullivan Bell Hamilton Graham Shuknecht Fisher Cooley Dickes Miller Randall Oliver Mannings
Mickey Rinehart Burg Vaughn Kibler Plowe Post Mooney MaCarthy Maxon Farrington Fisk English Crammer

153

Kohler Clifford Bommer Willard Ryan Esten Butler Legg Drilling Duncan Lamb Powell Hymphrey Bartlett
Mills Arena Sears Bowan Schneider Riner Clark Dunn Frank Gott Blackmore Baker Carney Majors Kennedy
Lewis Newcomb Osmanski Page Noble Orlando Moore Levy Ford Dougherty Driscoll Buck Brown Allen Benzs
Cole Booth Robinson Joslin Jones Merrill Hayes Phillips Stephens Wallace Uhl Peck Holbrook Anderson
Gilbert Knapp Alexander Wilbur Wing Zimmerman Lasch Marble Dempsey Herman Onisk Relyea Reed Hubbard
Nugent Nearhood Crawford Fisher Edwards Jessup Lee Blanding Austin Sellers Sommer Wagenhalls Sharpe
Speers Cotton Zimmer Gleason Richards Campbell Walton Bennet Cappotelli Graves Eichenberger Getners
Fritz Horan McMillan Merklinger Whitcomb Stokes Austen Richardson Boyd Daley Arnold Prentice Lennox
Paul Silver Tuttle Weiss Welch Norton Mack Brockmeier Heldstab Battaglia Copeland Carmichael Linton
Warfel Ferris Neidrauer Henrys Chamberlin Bacon Bailey Morgan Hawkes Ireland Kaiser McMaster Victor

Conroy Hodges Dennis Morris Chase Fox Hoag Tallman Collins Mason Salway Logan Spencer Hill Crow Ahl
Ditzel Parry Ward Sweet Kettle MacPherson Page Sargent York Burns Warboys Crawford Goodrich Emmerys
Goldsmith Cood Gleason Delplato White Hopkins Embury Mitchell Stamp Wagner Timothy Bryant Green Nye
Price Tiede Collier Zeh Jackson Curtiss Fleishman Atlanta Parks Ames Spaulding Doty Costello Gibson
Tubbs Day Berry Wiggins Beecher Crossett Dwyer Eaton Rowe Stevens Sukoski Appleby Barrett Youngmann
Griffen Shraeder Rodgers Metcaff Meier Howes Ford Dixon Elle Abbott Whitman Waggonner Whiteman Lang
Lucas Leo McGraw Addison Grant Fisher Fairchild Christie Buckeye Bailey Monroe North Petrone Peters
Pond Sullivan Rolston Vaughn Turner Meredith Normandy LaValley Hubbard Fish McDonald Crowell Curran
Fletcher May DeWitt Copeland Dejoy Burnette Edgar Jones Barber Radnor Downs Bishop Jones Akers Bank
Jones James Johnson Jackson Jerome Dewitt DiFlippo Demus Davis Deroo Baxter Beaver

APPENDIX B

1. The following Receipt Adjustment record contains commodities sold by or returned to a food processing plant. Make the appropriate program planning card, create and verify the tape file.

2. The following problem contains records in two formats:

   Format 1 contains commodity information (and a 1 in position 1)

   Format 2 contains the quantity shipped and customer information (and a 2 in position 1)

   Make the appropriate program planning card, create and verify the tape files.

(DUP)
Positions 1-2
XX

Date 8/7/73

Receipt Adjustment

(Numeric) Commodity #							(DUP) Date							(Alpha) Type			(LØ) Quantity				Sign -,+	(LØ) Dollars/Cents						Sign +,-	SKIP									
3	4	5	6	7	8	9	10	11	12	13	14	15	16	17	18	19	20	21	22	23	24	25	26	27	28	29	30	31	32	33	34	35	36	37	38	39	40
3	6	8	4	9	2	1								A	3	1	1	Ø	Ø	Ø	+		7	8	5	2	Ø	+									
3	6	8	5	Ø	Ø	4								Z	W	#			7	5	+		1	Ø	2	4	5	+									
3	7	8	Ø	4	2	1								V	8	A		1	Ø	Ø	+	1	Ø	5	7	6	2	+									
3	8	9	Ø	1	1	Ø								S	R	I			5	Ø	+			8	9	5	Ø	+									
4	Ø	6	Ø	9	1	8								A	4	2			9	5	-		2	3	8	7	6	-									
4	Ø	7	2	3	6	1								B	X	W	5	Ø	Ø	Ø	+	9	8	5	6	2	2	+									
5	1	3	2	7	6	4								1	3	F		1	Ø	Ø	+		3	8	5	7	6	+,									
5	2	2	2	3	8	1								D	Ø	6			5	Ø	+			6	4	1	7	+									
5	4	7	8	3	2	Ø								B	X	W			7	5	+			8	3	2	1	+									
6	9	9	8	7	4	9								V	8	2		1	Ø	Ø	+		4	2	6	5	0	+									

Commodity #	Description	Unit Price
A32XZ	Chairs	$ 12.00

	Quantity	Customer Name	Customer Address
	75	Albion Schools	Albion, New York
	7	Jones Bakery	Trenton, New Jersey
	24	Pullinzi Funeral Home	Ellicottville, Vermont

Commodity #	Description	Unit Price
B641R	Tables	$ 30.00

	Quantity	Customer Name	Customer Address
	100	Jamestown Community College	Jamestown, New York
	16	Xerox Corporation	Rochester, New York
	36	Candlelight Cafe	Springfield, Ohio

Commodity #	Description	Unit Price
C792F	Eggs	$ .98/doz.

	Quantity	Customer Name	Customer Address
	50 doz.	Loblaws	Attica, New York
	10 doz.	Joan'e Deli	Tonawanda, New York
	100 doz.	Tops Market	Batavia, New York

Commodity #	Description	Unit Price
D25CF	Test tubes	$ .75

	Quantity	Customer Name	Customer Address
	2000	University of California	Berkely, California
	400	Erie County Health Dept.	Buffalo, New York
	1200	Eastman Kodak	Dallas, Texas

Commodity #	Description	Unit Price
E427X	Roses	$ 8.00/doz.

	Quantity	Customer Name	Customer Address
	25 doz.	McConnell Florists	Akron, Ohio
	36 doz.	Floral Haven	Johnstown, Pennsylvania
	8 doz.	Flower Boutique	Hamilton, Ontario, Canada

INDEX

V

Verification, 135-37
  correction of errors during,
      88-89, 129-31
  data on tape, 14
  program loading of, 105-7
  records of, 83-99
  run, deletion of records during,
      95-98, 134-35

Verification *(Contd.)*
  tape error recovery during, 87
  tape movement during, 85-86

Z

Zero-fill, left, 75-76
Zipcode drill, 151

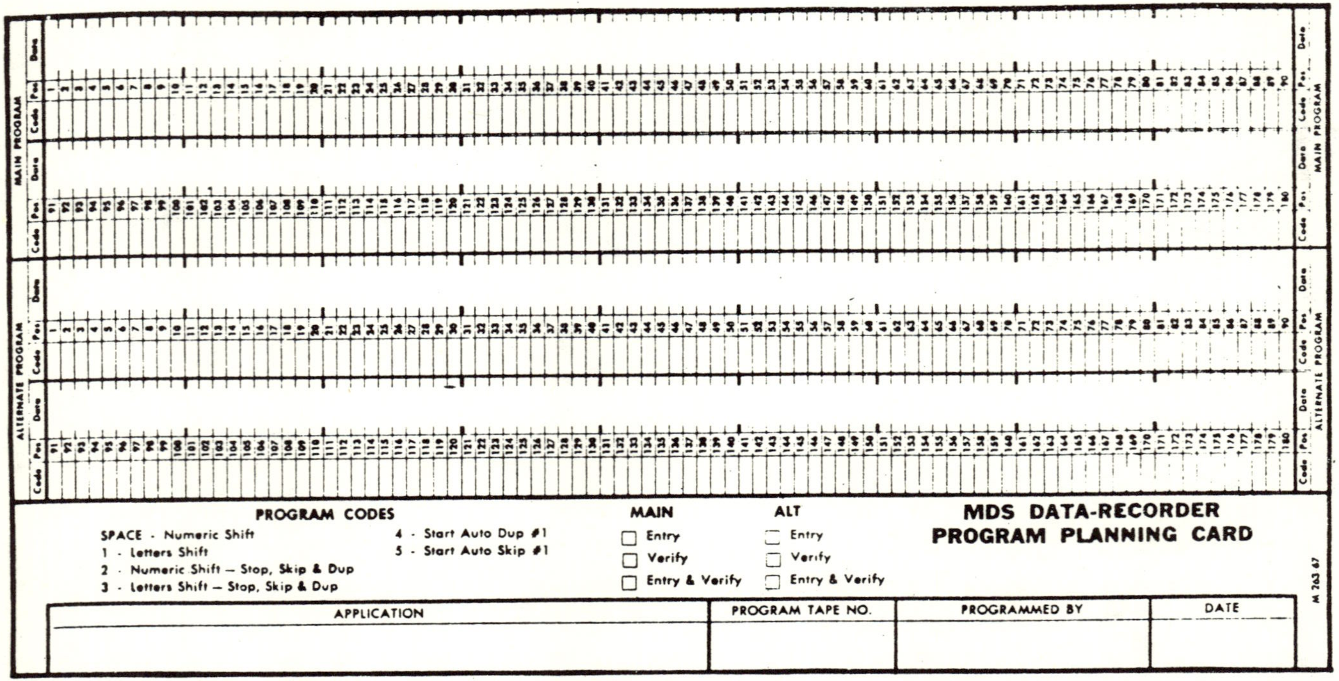

MDS DATA-RECORDER
PROGRAM PLANNING CARD

PROGRAM CODES

SPACE - Numeric Shift

1 - Letters Shift

2 - Numeric Shift — Stop, Skip & Dup

3 - Letters Shift — Stop, Skip & Dup

4 - Start Auto Dup #1

5 - Start Auto Skip #1

MAIN	ALT
☐ Entry	☐ Entry
☐ Verify	☐ Verify
☐ Entry & Verify	☐ Entry & Verify

PROGRAM TAPE NO.

APPLICATION

PROGRAMMED BY

DATE

M 263 67

MAIN PROGRAM — Code Pos. Date

ALTERNATE PROGRAM — Code Pos. Date

MDS DATA-RECORDER
PROGRAM PLANNING CARD

M 263 67

MAIN
- ☐ Entry
- ☐ Verify
- ☐ Entry & Verify

ALT
- ☐ Entry
- ☐ Verify
- ☐ Entry & Verify

PROGRAM TAPE NO.

PROGRAMMED BY

DATE

APPLICATION

PROGRAM CODES

SPACE - Numeric Shift
1 - Letters Shift
2 - Numeric Shift — Stop, Skip & Dup
3 - Letters Shift — Stop, Skip & Dup
4 - Start Auto Dup #1
5 - Start Auto Skip #1

MAIN PROGRAM — Code | Pos. | Data | Code | Pos. | Data

ALTERNATE PROGRAM — Code | Pos. | Data | Code | Pos. | Data

MDS DATA-RECORDER
PROGRAM PLANNING CARD

PROGRAM CODES

SPACE - Numeric Shift
1 - Letters Shift
2 - Numeric Shift — Stop, Skip & Dup
3 - Letters Shift — Stop, Skip & Dup
4 - Start Auto Dup #1
5 - Start Auto Skip #1

MAIN
☐ Entry
☐ Verify
☐ Entry & Verify

ALT
☐ Entry
☐ Verify
☐ Entry & Verify

APPLICATION	PROGRAM TAPE NO.	PROGRAMMED BY	DATE

ALTERNATE PROGRAM						MAIN PROGRAM					
Code	Pos	Data	Code	Pos	Data	Code	Pos	Data	Code	Pos	Data

M 263 67